Ends in......

By Bezzo

CONTENTS

CHAPTER ONE –
THE WORST DAY

Friday 9th April 2021, 12.25 pm, the worst day of my life. Those deafening words 'take him down' echoed through the courtroom. I couldn't even bring myself to look at my Brother-in-law (who had attended court with me) the shame, hurt, remorse and hatred I felt about myself was far too immense.

The Judge wasn't joking, down and down we went, staircase after staircase. We finally reached the basement of the courtroom. I couldn't control my emotions. The reality of what I had done, the people I had hurt, I just wanted to end it all.

In the courtroom basement, valuables are removed, bagged up, and quickly taken away. Sheer panic starts to take over, I feel numb, my whole body begins to shake. I felt like I was intoxicated and was experiencing some form of detox. I had no idea what the future holds for me.

I had a short visit from my Barrister and Solicitor. They explained that although I was sentenced to 14 months, this has been reduced to seven with remission, reduced by half again for good behaviour and released on tag. 426 days reduced to 107 almost seemed doable. The Barrister and Solicitor left. The guards wanted me taken from the court to prison as quickly as possible. At 12.45 pm I was in the court by 2.00pm I was on my way to Leicester CAT B Remand Prison. The fear of what lies ahead is terrifying.

On my way to the prison which is only a few miles from the court, I focused on the moving traffic, pedestrians crossing the roads, people just getting on with their daily lives. What I would do to turn the clock back. So many times, I have passed by those enormous gates leading into the prison, today I was actually going through them to be locked away from the outside world for the next 14 weeks or so.

The Sprinter van comes to a halt. We spend approximately 30 minutes in the yard waiting for my turn to be welcomed into the Custody Suite. I am eventually taken out of the van to be welcomed by a beautiful black Labrador, a trained sniffer dog checking for drugs. I got the all clear and was allowed in.

I could see that the guards were very busy, I was put in a cell at approximately 2.30 pm, Friday afternoon. Welcome to the weekend, all alone in a cell with nothing but my thoughts and a toilet for company. All I could focus on was what would be the best and quickest way to end it all here and now. Surveying the room, everything was bolted down, nothing free standing. Toilet roll was the only available item, it was so thin you could put your fingers through it, hardly going to be able to hang myself with it. The only other option was the zip on my trousers, could I slit my wrist, not sharp enough, not happening. Looks like I am here for the foreseeable future.

Around 5.00 pm the cell door opens, "come on Beresford" said one of the guards dressed all in black with a white shirt and all tooled up. The guard took me into a side room and told me to strip off and get dressed into the new 2021 strip (I wish). There was a pair of grey joggers, grey t-shirt/sweatshirt, grey socks and wait for it blue boxers, wow, nice!!

"Hold your hands out" the guard said. He handed over a plastic sack containing bedding, more grey clothing and 'let's get ready to rumble' plimsoles. "What size" the guard asks, I replied "size 12", "too big, put your shoes back on" he replied. There I stood in my grey prison gear with my Sunday best shoes on. An image that will never be forgotten. I was shown back to my cell.

At Approximately 6.00 pm a Nurse appears. She escorted me to another room where there we're two other Nurses. My height and weight are checked. Lots of questions and paperwork to be completed. The Nurse asks if I have any other medical concerns/issues. "Yes, how about I just want to end it all and kill myself" I replied. The Nurse knew that I was being serious. She replied "this is not good, we will have to open an Act", whatever one of those is? This meant a lot more questions which needed to be asked by a more senior member of staff. After answering all the necessary questions. I was put on 15-minute observation checks and suicide watch.

It is now 7.30pm – time to face the music. I was being taken to the induction wing, where I would be allowed one phone call. Three other lads arrived back from court. They were quite jovial, joking with each other over their sentence of 18 years. I had no idea how I was going to deal with 14 weeks let alone 18 years. We were taken through a tunnel of numerous locked doors, outside, inside, more doors. Finally, we reached the wing. I felt physically sick and terrified of how I was going to deal with being locked up and felt completely alone.

It was a very old Victorian style wing, with lots of bars and cell doors with rifle slots in for easy viewing. I was asked more questions by the wing officers. I was handed more items including a breakfast pack, tea and coffee. I was escorted to my cell which was to be my luxury accommodation for the foreseeable future. A quaint little room with bunk beds with a mattress about 4 inches thick, some old Formica furniture, a small tv, a kettle and a heater which was like a tube of plastic cups from a vending machine, the cell was approximately 5m x 2.5m. There was a small window (with a sea view – NOT). The walls were dingy, the floor cold. My thoughts were running wild. 'I can't do this' were the words that just kept repeating over and over again in my head.

Finally, what I had been waiting for, a 3-minute phone call to someone was permitted. I desperately wanted to speak to my beautiful wife. My court case was initially scheduled for 3.30pm. My wife had gone to work and planned to be home for 12.30 pm to see me before I attended court. I received a phone call at 11.00 am from my Solicitor to inform me that my court hearing had been bought forward to 12.30 pm. It was too late for My wife to get home to see me before I left for court. How was she going to react after hearing the news that I had been given a custodial sentence? I had no idea. The officer dialled the number and handed me the phone. My wife answered. I could hear by her voice she was crying. What was I going to say in 3 minutes? There was lots of tears, anger and sorrow. No warning that my three minutes were up. The line went dead. I was absolutely devastated I didn't even get to say goodbye. I placed down the receiver and was taken back to my cell. The cell door was closed behind me and locked. I have never felt so alone. No-one to talk to, feeling like I had ruined everything. I had hurt and let down everyone I cared about. Was my wife going to stand by me? Can she ever forgive me? Do I have a future with her? I could not switch off. The realisation of what I had done and the punishment hits home. I just wanted to end it now. It's going to be a long night with just me and my thoughts.

I decided to take the bottom bunk bed. I make my bed, emptied my kit bag and made myself a cup of tea. My stomach was churning, I could not bring myself to eat anything. Lights off, I laid down, the bed was so uncomfortable to say the least. My heart was pounding, the hustle and bustle of guards moving around on the wing, constantly putting a torch to the opening in the cell door to check that I had not harmed myself.

The night seemed to last forever, tossing and turning. Impossible to get comfortable sleeping on such a thin mattress it felt like I was sleeping on solid wood.

It's Saturday morning, 10th April 2021. I was in an extremely bad way mentally. I could not stop thinking about my wife, what I had done to her, she didn't deserve any of this. She has been nothing but the perfect wife. How could I have been so selfish and ruin everything we had. I had no appetite, the thought of food made me feel physically sick, I managed to stomach a cup of tea. It wasn't long before officers came to check on my wellbeing. They could tell I was in a bad way and immediately summoned for the Nurse. She spent a significant amount of time with me talking about my feelings. My blood pressure was though the roof, they didn't seem to know which way to turn. They decided to keep me under observation. I was asked if I wanted a shower, which I agreed to. I was informed that due to my state of mind they would allow me another phone call to my wife.

Heading to the shower block I ran into a young inmate called Dean (not his real name), he glanced at me, and asked "what you in for" I replied "fraud". I reciprocated the question, he relied "murder". He appeared so young, probably around 25 years old. He said he was on remand awaiting trial in Cambridge. I thought to myself 'he is facing years in prison if found guilty'. I am facing 14 weeks, it started to put thing into some perspective that I could be out in just over 3 months. I arrived at the shower block. There were three showers in a row with screens waist high between each one. I took the middle shower. I expected the shower to be cold or possibly luke warm but it was surprisingly quite hot.

Next was my phone call to my wife. I was feeling nervous, I didn't know what to expect. Did we have a future together, was she going to stand by me? Was this the end of my marriage? The phone rang she answered almost immediately. We made the most of the 3 minutes, she was obviously still angry, hurt and felt let down, but supportive beyond belief. Suddenly I thought I can hopefully get through this and try to put things right and get back to some form of normal life. My wife had without a shadow of doubt, just saved my life. The phone bleeped, a sign the call was about to end. I told my wife I loved her and we said our goodbyes.

After my call, I was whisked away to a side room. There were two officers and two mental health workers waiting for me to discuss how I was feeling, focusing on the suicidal thoughts. After speaking to my wife, I had a change of heart. Life is going to be worth living. I can get through this and make a fresh start. I owe it to her. I am still young enough to enjoy my life. If my wife is prepared to give me a chance to prove myself, what more could I ask for! I want us to grow old together, I want to look after her and protect her. The mental health workers were happy with the conversation and my change of heart and decided to remove the Act which meant I was no longer on suicide watch. I had to accept what I had done, and accept this was my punishment. I started to think positive thoughts which put me in a much better frame of mind. It wasn't going to be easy but I am up for the challenge.

CHAPTER TWO – THE WEEKEND

It's Saturday night, 10th April 2021, I am feeling completely alone, isolated in a confined space with my thoughts running away with me. My heart starts racing again, panic starts to kick in. I feeling scared so I decide to buzz for help. Bad decision, a foreign girl appeared speaking very poor English she promptly departed. No sign of a Nurse. It suddenly came to me that it was the weekend and I assumed there must have been a change of staff and that possibly very little happens over the weekend. I finally managed to drift off to sleep.

Sunday 11th April 2021 beckons, its day three and I am really not feeling great. My mood has deteriorated rapidly over night. I knew I was not going to be allowed a call today. A Nurse finally arrived mid-morning. I had requested help 18 hours ago; anything could have happened to me during that time. The Nurse was pleasant and seemed to want to help. She examined me. I had pain in my stomach. She asked if I had gallstones. I replied "no idea, not that I know of". She said that gallstones could be the problem here. She stated that I would need to see a doctor urgently tomorrow (Monday) or Tuesday. The Nurse left. I tried to calm myself down and focus on positive thoughts. I accepted that it was going to be a long-drawn-out day! I was wrong – next thing I hear the jangling of keys, an officer unlocks and opens the door "you want a mate Beresford" he asked. I replied with "do I have a choice". To my amazement the officer replied "yes you do" I replied "what if I don't" The office replied with "you want to meet the Governor and go on report?". That is something that I did not want to experience so I agreed to having another inmate sharing my cell.

My new inmate arrived. His name was Tad. First, I thought that is a good local name, how wrong I was. He was from Vietnam, only 24 years old. He spoke very little English, in fact, virtually next to none. Top bunk for him. I was somewhat intrigued to hear how a young man from the other side of the world had ended up as my cell mate.

He tried to explain to me that he was staying for one night only in a property in Leicester, when the house was raided by the police. Amazingly they had found a cannabis farm on the first floor, which he said he knew nothing about. I have to admit I wasn't convinced, and obviously neither was the Magistrate. He said he was due to appear at the Crown Court in May. It took a long time for him to explain his situation due to his poor English, however, it was someone to talk to and it certainly passed the time away. Now this conversation was out of the way I decided to see what was on TV. There were only 12 channels to choose from. I switched the TV on and Harry Potter came on. Not a fan of Harry Potter really not the sort of film I would normally watch but my new lodger seemed to understand what it was and became excited and wanted to watch it. I left him to it, it couldn't do any harm to make him feel comfortable around me. It was a double bill, four hours long!! School boy error, however, there was a method in my madness as I wanted to watch Line of Duty and Match of the Day later that evening.

I am a massive Arsenal supporter. Arsenal have not been having the greatest of seasons, however, amazingly they won 3-0 away at Sheffield. I knew Sheffield were bottom of the league and you would expect Arsenal to win but 3 points to Arsenal and a clean sheet bought a smile to my face. That was a result and a good end to the day. Now time to try and get some sleep, if only I could switch off and make myself comfortable it would help.

It's Monday 12ᵗʰ April 2021. I wake early and make myself a cup of tea. There appears to be guards and staff running around all over the place. All having their own unique jobs to do. The cell door opens "exercise anyone" "No thanks" I replied. The door bangs closed and locked. The door is unlocked and opened again. A Nurse appears "covid test" "Another" I replied. As far as I was concerned this was my passport and the next step to be transferred from the induction wing to the main wing. There was no argument from me. The covid test was all done. Another Nurse appeared, I realised this was the Nurse that had been to see me yesterday with regards to the gallstones and high blood pressure. Blood pressure checked. 140/100. Still high. I have never known my blood pressure to be this high before.

I was hoping that I would be allowed to call my wife again today. How wrong was I! The office was closed and no contact numbers for me had been activated yet. My mood suddenly dropped. This was totally out of my control. I just have to wait and try again tomorrow. Thanks for nothing!!

So, that was the first weekend over, I have a long way to go. I have to focus on getting through one day at a time. I decided to make a calendar and mark each day off. I thought this might help me to mentally see that every day I am in here is a day closer to me being released. The realisation that the weekends are going to be hard (as everything seems to come to a standstill) hit home. I need to focus on something to keep my mind occupied.

It's Tuesday 13ᵗʰ April 2021. I wake up early. I cannot lay in this bed feeling sorry for myself. I need some sort of plan, something to focus on. My days need to be structured otherwise I am going to go insane. I decide to start exercising. Being a qualified Personal Trainer, surely. I know enough exercises that I can do without any equipment. I could exercise twice a day, once in the morning and once in the evening. At least this will pass some of the time away. Nice and simple to begin with. I devise a routine, a hundred lunges and curls followed by a couple of planks, some sit-ups and stretches. Maybe I could manage to shed a few pounds while in here, it certainly won't do me any harm to lose a bit of weight.

My mindset had started to changed. I have to be prepared for whatever may come next. Whatever I decide to do with my day isn't going to take away the guilt and shame that I am feeling but hopefully I can help myself to make my time in here go quicker. I presume the day will start with a shower, then I can exercise and hopefully get a phone call to my wife. I heard the jingling of keys, the door opened "come on Beresford, health centre and visit to the Doctor for you" a guard said.

Over the past few months, I have experienced a number of health issues, depression, anxiety, the feeling of heart racing constantly. I have contacted my registered GP Surgery and spoken to numerous Doctors about how I am feeling, I have never felt such desperation for help. However, due to the pandemic no-one can attend the Surgery therefore no face-to-face interaction possible. How can anyone really see and understand how I am feeling without actually seeing me.

First thoughts were at least it gets me out of this cell, a short walk and maybe a bit of fresh air. Led by the guard I am taken through another tunnel of locked doors, even when we went outside it continued with lock door after lock door. I was starting to feel like a convicted murderer. Finally, I actually get to see a doctor in the flesh. She examined me, she confirmed that I did not have any heart problems but I possibly have gallstones. Tablets and a scan are the Doctors recommendation. In just over 30 minutes of seeing a doctor face-to-face I had a diagnosis which was more than I received from my own GP in 4 months. If anything positive could come out of being in this awful place, getting my health sorted would be a result.   It was a nice trip out taking everything into consideration. Back to my luxury apartment now, just in time to be allowed to go for a shower. All I really wanted to lift my moral now was to phone my wife. How wrong could I be. No phone call allowed again today. This sent my emotions into turmoil. I just needed to speak to my wife. I needed to check that she was OK. I had not had any contact since my 3-minute call last Saturday. We are Husband and Wife, we are a team, my best mate. All I wanted was to hear her voice to help me get through the day. I thought about how distraught she must be feeling. Again, the realisation of what I had done bought a knot to my stomach. Waiting for the next call was not going to be good for my Mental Health. I know how worried my wife was about my Mental Health. I knew that she would be worried and concerned due to my on-going suicidal thoughts. However, I knew that she knew I was OK she would also cope better with this awful situation that I only had myself to blame.

Not being able to speak to my wife the panic started to set in again and the suicidal thoughts started to return. I couldn't accept and live with myself for what I had done, no contact was driving me insane. I demanded a 3-minute call, I explained how desperate I was. In the end my request was granted. My wife wasn't good. I could tell by her voice she was struggling. She was trying to tell me she was OK, but I knew she was far from OK. I just needed to know that she was going to be waiting for me on my release. Without her I had nothing to focus on, no future, my life was over. The 3-minutes went really quickly, we were cut off. I didn't even get to say 'goodbye'. At least I had heard her voice that was good enough for now. It was enough to settle my anxiety down. At least I was hopeful I may be able to get some sleep tonight.

Wednesday started with a delivery, a thick A4 envelope. 'What goodies are in here I wonder'. It was an Education Pack containing form after form which I was expected to complete including a Maths and English test. They wanted to know where I would sit on the idiot's scale. The tests weren't difficult. I completed all the questions and returned the forms within the hour. At least this was another distraction to pass some time away.

Another surprise as the cell door opened. A middle-aged lady stood in the doorway "book from the library for you" she said. It was a word search puzzle book. I am not really into reading and puzzles but instantly I thought it would be another distraction. Beggars can't be choosers in here! Sudoku is my forte. My wife will often comment on how quickly I complete a Sudoku puzzle. Off the lady trotted. However, she returned in 5 minutes with a book called 'Ambush' written by James Patterson. OK, I thought, let's start reading.

5 pm everyday was what I called the 'walk of shame'. It was time to collect your dinner, most of the guards would just stand around and watch, surely there was no need but I suppose it had to be done, checking to ensure that no-one stepped out of line. Order something solid for dinner to try to fill me up until lights out was my intention. I am not used to eating my dinner so early. Around 6.30 pm was the norm for me. my definition of solid was way off the mark the dinner was nothing more than a plate of 'slops'. My roommate's dinner went straight down the toilet. There was no way he was going to eat what was in front of him. I was soon quick to learn the daily routines and not to expect anything good. Anything good was going to be a bonus.

All I could hope for to finish the day off before being confined to my cell, was a call to my wife. It didn't happen. Everything crossed that I will be able to speak to her tomorrow.

CHAPTER THREE – PHONE REDEMPTION

Thursday arrives, I have survived my first week. It has been far from easy. Finally, after a lot of determination, constantly pressuring and raising my voice at the guards, my requested phone contact numbers are activated. I am ecstatic, I can call my wife. I think there was an element of a guilty conscience on behalf of the prison for not allowing me a phone call, for what had seemed like forever, as a guard arrives with the wing mobile phone and asks if I would like some privacy as this was my first official call home without a guard ringing the number and standing over me. I was left alone to phone home.

I cannot put into words the immense feeling of emotion running through my veins. I was allowed a call, convenient to me and for as long as my credit would last, I didn't have to clock watch for a measly 180 seconds before the line would go dead. I couldn't wait to hear my wife's voice. She didn't know that I was calling. 'I hope she answers' I felt anxious. I dialled the number. 'Please answer', she answered virtually straight away. We both had a job to speak at first. It didn't take long before we started to feel relaxed. To my absolute amazement she was going to stand by me and offer all the support that she possibly could. She did not condone in any way shape or form what I had done. However, it had been two years since the initial confession. We had had time to already put some things in place to stop me gambling. I remember her saying "you have a choice Nick, either a life with your wife or a life of gambling. "If you want to gamble you have to let me go". I replied with

"It is a no-brainer I am never putting myself, or you, through this again".

 I truly felt I didn't deserve any forgiveness, or expect my wife to be so determined to help me through this. I knew it would be difficult. How could she ever trust me again? I suppose trust comes with time and I will do everything to prove to her that I can change. She kept telling me that she was ok, however I wasn't sure that I believed her, but how was I going to know any different. I just had to keep believing that she was OK. Previously, when life had been tough and unbearable, I had taken solitude by visiting a lake full of ducks and swans, armed with a loaf or three of bread, it always seemed to work for me. There was nowhere, being stuck in here, where I could have that solitude.

For some reason I started to think about my father who passed away when I was in my 30's. When the new Emirates stadium was built, stones were laid for loved ones. The Grandchildren had placed one in memory of him. This is my special place which I like to visit when life is difficult (especially being one of Arsenals biggest fans). Perhaps a trip to the Emirates to have a chat with Dad, on my release will do me good.

When you are rock bottom and life feels like not living, it is amazing how just hearing that my wife is going to stand by me and support me, gives me some hope that I can get through this. The days in here can seem very long at times. I have learnt very quickly that time must be embraced and you have to hold on to the thought that every day is another day closer to me walking out of this god- forsaken place. I have to make it to the end for my wife, all the family and friends who are supporting me in what I can only describe as the worse experience of my life.

The weekend was upon us and I was starting to feel in a better place. It is early Saturday morning and my mind starts reflecting on the past few days What a week though, never to be forgotten I might add and the old adage comes to mind that you always find out who your friends are in difficult times. Fridays seem like a day of madness. Phone calls were allowed (thank goodness), but no showers, how inhumane. Having a shower was at least a way of getting out of the cell, passing some time away and just seeing another face (although I never felt scared or intimidated about my own safety). It was as if Friday was the day the courts would be busy and the inmate count would grow significantly, however, there were as many leaving as there was arriving. After all Leicester Prison is a remand prison. Once sentenced inmates can be moved anywhere in the Country. I was starting to feel like an old face in here, keeping myself to myself and keeping my head down was the safest way to protect yourself. I could understand how some inmates seem to accept Prison as the norm. The thought of how anyone could survive mentally was beyond me.

Today both Tad and me have our second covid lateral flow test. If the tests are negative apparently, we could be moved into the main Prison wing. (I wasn't sure if this was good or bad news) The reality of the weeks ahead suddenly came to the forefront of my mind. The anxiety started to kick in. However, at least if both of us received negative results we would be moved together, which was something. Any internal correspondence/mail was delivered anytime from 10.00 pm. All we could do was wait! I assume this was a job carried out by the night shift staff. Finally late evening, we received good news both Tad and myself were negative; a move onto the main wing was on the cards. However, I doubt anything will happen over the weekend. Although for inmates the weekend was no different to every other day of the week, a phone call, shower, meal and lock up. At least tonight we had the FA.CUP Semi Final to look forward to - Chelsea v Man City. We settled down to watch the game. Huge build up for the game - what a disappointment. Over the years I have watched loads of football matches of all levels. This game was awful, I wish I hadn't bothered. It was one of the worst FA. Cup Semi Finals I have ever seen; exciting was an understatement; it was complete rubbish.

Today was pretty much the same shower, phone call and dinner. The highlight of every day is talking to my wife. Every day I hear her voice is another day closer to us being re-united. I want to know everything, how she is doing, what are her plans for today, how is she feeling? Just knowing that she is OK and coping is enough to help me to get through the day. I make the call. I can always tell by her voice that she is hurting, but she remains so calm and positive about our future. I think we both have the same thought. If my wife knows that I am coping she can get through her day and vice versa. The call always ends with us both saying "I love you" then it's back to the cell to see out yet again another long weekend.

Time for a shower, interesting place. Three showers in a line with dividers waist high, nothing left to the imagination. You just do what you have to do and move on. There is another inmate in the shower, a lad called Patrick, we exchange pleasantries, which is always a good feeling. It's when there are unpleasantries that you need to watch your back. Turns out he's in for 21 years, somebody caught him on a bad day. The general rule in here seems to be never to ask "what you in for", wasn't politically correct. The rest of the day is pretty much the same, boring, just watching the hours pass by.

A new week begins Monday 19th April. Being covid clear must be time to leave the induction wing. How right I was, no sooner had the buzz of a Monday morning begun, when the door opened, there was a youngish guard standing in the doorway "you two get yourselves sorted, everything together, fifteen minutes and we are moving to the wing". Tad still half asleep, an expression of shock on his face "what's happening" he asked. He seemed far from happy, he became anxious, I could tell by his body language that he was not looking forward to being on the main wing, and to be honest, the unexpected started to hit home. However, whatever lay ahead I had his back, being on remand in a foreign country, very poor understanding of the language and being banged up with an Arsenal fan, must have been daunting to say the least. He must be thinking "could things get any worse". He seemed harmless, probably been promised this great new life in England and here he was at HMP Leicester. Exploitation is probably the long and short of his story.

Off we went, escorted by the guard, to the main wing. It was hardly a stone's throw away from where we had been remanded for the last week, but hey ho. The guard opened the cell door "all clean and ready for you" he said. I took one look at the cell I replied "who by I asked "Stevie Wonder"? I accepted that I don't deserve luxury but this was disgusting to say the least. If this was going to be my home for the next 12 weeks, I had to clean it from top to bottom. At least it should be clean for new inmates. Tad helped and we made it as clean as possible - it had to be right. Tad was struggling he did not seem to understand what was happening. I tried to explain this was the next part of the process. It was far from easy to get through to him. I felt his pain. He is finally Settling down. A letter was posted through the door it was addressed to Tad. It was from his Solicitor, which he could not read let alone understand. I got him to sit down with me. I started to explain as best as I could the content of his letter. It stated that he was to appear in Leicester Crown Court on Monday 17th May. He became really emotional and looked so alone. I felt so desperately sorry for him. Being in here, alone, in a foreign county, he had five weeks wondering what his future fate was going to be. Reading between the lines, deportation was a distinct possibility; from a completely selfish point of view, I felt comfortable around him. I could offer him help and support to get through this awful time. It felt like we were going to be OK together. He was, in the grand scale of things, a good cellmate to have. I can take my mind off my own mental health issues and focus on helping him through. It will certainly help to pass the time away. Things could have been a lot worse for us both. We could have both been sharing a cell with a murderer!!

Once we had settled in it was time to call my wife which was the order of the day. I explained the day's events. I knew today was going to be a really difficult day for her. She was heading into work for the first time since the bombshell. Having not disclosed what she was going through, to her employers, or any of her colleagues. My court case had hit the press. This was always her biggest nightmare, if it got into the press. She knew that the gossip would spread like wildfire. She was right. She was inundated with text messages. I totally understood that she felt nothing but hurt, embarrassment, shame, and most of all being let down by me, her husband. I felt so sorry, I wasn't even going to be with her when she got home to be there for her. I was no use whatsoever. The hatred I felt about myself started to bring back the thoughts of ending it all. The only thing I could do was go over and over in my head that she was going to be there for me when I got released. I pulled myself together. I knew she would turn to family and friends if she needed to. The desperation to speak to her again to check she was ok was nothing less than unbearable. All I could do was hope that tomorrow came quickly.

I assumed the wing would be much the same as the induction but there were different guards working on the wing which I had not seen before. They seemed to have their own ways of how the wing was managed, which was something we were going to have to get used to. However, the meals were exactly the same though, no improvement. We had to accept that even the food wasn't going to be something we could look forward to. We soon learnt that we were allowed to exercise Monday & Tuesday at 9am and Wednesday & Thursday at 2.30pm. No exercise allowed on Fridays, then Saturday afternoons and Sunday morning were routine. Ok I thought, at least I enjoy exercise and this would help pass time away, with the exception of Fridays which I had to accept was going to be a long-drawn-out day, confined to the cell. The yard was the way to get out into the open and take in some fresh air.

Time for a shower. Heading off to the showers, which were virtually the same set up as on the induction wing, I was joined by a lad;

we pass pleasantries, he introduced himself as Sam. We briefly chatted. He was being released at the end of the week. He told me his wife had cheated on him and he took his anger out on the perpetrator. But then what bloke, in the heat of the moment, wouldn't perhaps? I would feel like doing the same. I wished him well and headed back to my cell.

I hadn't been back in my cell long when there was that dreaded sound of the jangling of keys. The cell door opened. A Nurse entered "blood pressure" she said. My blood pressure was checked, the reading was reasonable, finally going down. It was 135/95. I took a sigh of relief, hopefully the concerns over my health were starting to subside. The Nurse was pleased, told me to take care of myself and left. I had every intention of keeping my head down and looking after myself. However, my mental health was not good. I needed to focus on doing something to pass the time away until I was released and back with my wife where I belong. Being away from her was the most difficult part of this. The love I have for her is priceless, how I had let her down constantly played on my mind. The less time I had for thinking, the quicker the days would pass. I needed some structure. I decided to do some writing, something I had not really done before. Finally, the days will come to an end.

Monday evening is when you can order goods from the canteen. Basically, a list full of wonderful supermarket choices. All inmates have money credited to their prison accounts. You were allowed £5 for telephone calls and £3.50 for canteen per week (if your account has built up and you were more than £25 in credit you received no phone credit). Also loved ones could send money to you which would automatically be credited to your account. If you are lucky enough to get a job you are paid extra up to £1.50 per day if you worked in the kitchen. This would also be credited to your canteen account. All goods order on a Monday were delivered on Friday. At least we had something to look forward to on a Friday. The excitement; I could hardly contain myself.

CHAPTER FOUR
- SURPRISED

I have been here, stuck in here, for well into two weeks now, how time flies when you're having fun, not. The wing at times, especially at night, was quite noisy. I never really know why, the cell is situated on the first floor, so there were cells above and below me I decided to investigate where the noise was coming from and what the problem was. The second floor appeared to the same as ours, what I would describe as a normal wing, whatever one of those may be. I will leave that to your imagination. Believe you me, it is not something that I would recommend to anyone and something I never want to experience again. The ground floor is slightly different, it is split into sections, the centre being the kitchen servery area, the opposite end being some sort of segregation area and directly beneath our cell was another section. This apparently was called the isolation wing, specifically for inmates who decide to cause trouble. I thought this was a little too close for comfort, which did make me feel uneasy. However, after further investigation it became apparent that the isolation wing is situated in the basement but was being painted and therefore the troublesome inmates had been moved temporarily to the wing below. "Great" I thought. During the day there was just the occasional shout and door banging, but with a heavy guard presence, dressed all in black, with nice bomber hats on, the problems seemed less often and unnoticeable.

Tuesdays was another special day! The menus for the following week were delivered. Normally there we're 4 or 5 choices to pick from. The Lunchtime menu included a baguette, pasta pot or similar. The dinner menu consisted of a variety of choices. Dinner time was anytime between 4.30 – 5.30. I was quick to learn to select solids or items which they had to buy in, like pies or fish, anything that wasn't made by your fellow inmates, which resulted in a plate of slop. It was clearly a much better, and healthy option and possibly safer. You just never know who might add an unhealthy ingredient.

As the day passed, we moved into an unpredictable evening. The mood downstairs appears to be getting worse by the minute. It's that time of the evening when the day time staff hand over to the night time staff. The night shift staff must be getting briefed on the day-to-day comings and goings, which appears to be managed by a skeleton number of staff, and that is putting it mildly. But then you have to consider that the Prison has many wings to cover, including the isolation block of those troublesome inmates (naughty boys). We will come back to them later.

Right beneath us is an African guy with a very deep voice. I would guess he was probably in his 50's. His voice was so deep and loud it could be heard right through the prison. Everyone must have known which wing/cell he was in. Directly opposite him in cell 2-20, which was in full view of our cell, was a young Indian chap probably in his 30's. As the evening went on it literally became a war of words between the pair of them. There were lots of threats of violence being shouted between them, the banging became worse. It was almost if they were having a competition to see who could make the most noise.

This continued throughout the evening and late into the night. Tad was beside himself "if this was Vietnam the guards would go in and beat them to sleep" he said. Nice image came into my head, did this really happen in Vietnam? Furthermore, Tad said "if that didn't work, they would take them outside and just shoot them". Maybe some people would find this perhaps a bit harsh, but we could probably learn a thing or two from this, to stop inmates taking things into their own hands. Anyway, due to the night's entertainment, lethargy had set in and this morning, there wasn't a lot of get up and go from anyone.

Wednesday morning was very quiet, everyone looked exhausted and far from happy with the previous night's events. I thought to myself, if anyone gets hold of either of the culprits then it could get nasty, that was for sure. After a very quiet morning the afternoon arrived and we had a pleasant surprise, everyone on our floor was allowed outside for an hour's exercise 2.00 – 3.00 pm. At least this will break the afternoon up. It was a bright sunny day and I could enjoy exercising in the sun and get some fresh air. This was our first trip to the main exercise yard. Off we went through a couple of doors, then into what looked like a wire tunnel. When we reached the end of the tunnel, we entered the exercise yard which looked like it had once been a five a side football pitch. At the side there was an area for inmates to just stand and mooch around. Basically, everyone used it for whatever purpose they preferred. Some of the inmates utilise their time walking, others just sitting or standing in their little groups chatting. At all times you have to have your wits about you, you could sense that eyes were wandering and just knew they were checking each other out. Everybody was on their guard, watching their own backs. It was scary at times because, if anyone had decided to kick off, as you might say, there were only a couple of guards as security; it could end up being a bloodbath.

I initially walked around the viewing area. In my head I counted fifty steps, so if I did 50 laps that would work out to 2500 steps. A good exercise to add to my cell plan was my thought. Sunshine and walking; two of the things my wife and me enjoyed doing all the time together, this gave me a little bit of normality time. I thought about My wife; this helped to take my mind of this wretched situation that I had got myself into. At home, we would walk approximately 1000 steps every ten minutes, 6000 steps per hour. What was so surprising was that out of a group of approximately 35 inmates, only a couple were actually bothering to do any walking, with the majority just standing around chatting, exercising their jaws. Worse than a group of old women I thought. One thing was apparent though; in each group of men, there seemed to be jostling for leadership. Something I certainly did not want to be partied to.

That was it, exercise time was over for today and we are all instructed to head back to our cells. All that was left for us today to look forward to was an evening meal and hopefully a quiet night. The quietness didn't last for long; at around 5pm the African and Indian were at each other again, what a racket. They were squaring up to each other from behind closed doors. I wonder if they would behave in the same manner if they actually met face-to-face. Would they react the same or would they back off, especially if there was some of the other inmates around to keep things in order. This continues for the rest of the evening and well into the night/early hours of the morning.
Amazingly, the guards do absolutely nothing to intervene: they just let it continue, which just riled and annoyed all the other inmates, who just wanted to get some kip.

Our cell overlooked a small exercise yard which is usually used for any newcomers. I looked out of the cell window; through the bars there were half a dozen lads out for their morning exercise. It was around 8am. Our African friend below becomes involved in a heated exchange with them from his cell window, something I was going to have to get accustomed to. They were shouting back with no intervention from any of the guards "I'm gonna cut you up bad" I heard one of them shout. Lovely start to the morning. Again, it appeared they wanted to do serious harm to one another, is there really any need. Certain inmates seem to think the world owed them. As far as I was concerned, we were all in here for a reason. I had to accept that I had made a bad choice in life and this is my punishment, nobody owed me anything. I had all the hard work to do when I am released to put things right and apologise to those whom I had let down. The guards seem totally oblivious and didn't seem to want to get involved, that is ok but sooner or later someone will take it into their own hands and do their jobs for them and that could have devastating consequences.

Thursday is laundry day. The system was to place anything that you wanted washing in your wash bag and put out on the landing ready to be collected by the team from the laundry. Nice and simple strip your bed and send down your underpants, the jobs a good one. Washing was washed and dried really quickly and back at the cell by mid-afternoon, quality service, I thought. The washing of my underpants became a standing joke between my wife and me. I have never liked wearing boxers. The only pair of pants that I had were the ones I wore when I first came in. So, Friday was always a special day when I got to wear my favourite underpants. My wife joked that on my release the underpants were going in the bin!

I went for my daily afternoon exercise, another hour spent pounding around the yard. Pushing myself to hit 3000 steps in thirty minutes. Trouble is, the longer you are in here the more you get to pass pleasantries with other inmates and everyone wants you to stop and have a chat. There were even a couple of middle-aged Albanians, who I seemed to attract and seemed friendly enough. I had absolutely no intensions of upsetting or crossing anyone in here. I am reasonably tall, six foot and pretty well built with broad shoulders. Some of the lads just say "here comes the big fellow". I suppose I give the impression of the build of a rugby player. Although I have never really been into rugby, but a massive football fan. Obviously six foot and a well-built frame brings respect in a place like this. I just walk the yard, do not stop for anyone and it seems to work. I'm definitely not a trouble maker. I just want to do my time, keep my head down and get through this as safely as possible. Unfortunately, after completing today's walk, I ended up with a dead leg, I must have over done the walking, could I shake it off, near on impossible. I decided to speak to the nurse, who popped in and left me some pain killers, nurofen and paracetamol. Leaving me plenty to see me through the next few days. Interesting I thought firstly a good sign she trusted me to take them, but then only two weeks ago I was on suicide watch and I now had the ammunition to do just that. It was never going to happen though ruin my future with my wife I think not.

Laundry has arrived back all screwed up and thrown into our bags, lovely I thought. Straight out of the tumble drier still warm. At least we will have a nice clean bed to get into tonight, something everyone loves.

Thursday evening beckoned, what sort of night did we have to look forward to. I wondered. You could tell there was tension in the air downstairs, but a quiet evening for all of us. Then at about 4am everything went mad, our African friend was totally out of control. It sounded like a scene from the film "The Exorcist" all I could here was "Bitch, Bitch, Bitch". Over and over again, who this was being directed at I was unsure. In turn, this started our Indian friend off, who was on the opposite side of the wing. He was in demolition mode, that door was made of sterner stuff and was going nowhere. You would have to give him ten out of ten for effort though. Perhaps the guards thought they could leave them to burn themselves out, to our cost.

The new day arrives; everyone is feeling slightly weary, apart from a couple who are catching up on much needed sleep after that episode. Why do they do it and what are they hoping to achieve. Today is Friday 23rd April, two weeks down the line and feeling in a much better place than I did a fortnight ago. Looking forward to the future now with my beautiful wife, my wife. I'm paying the price having to spend all of this time apart from her. We have never really spent any time apart over the last decade, so this is hard for both of us. But it will never happen again.

CHAPTER FIVE - BIRTHDAYS

Friday is a mad day in here, no exercise, showers alternate weeks and in the afternoon your shopping is delivered, so any goodies ordered on a Monday should arrive today. It's a long time to be locked up; the prison blames covid and nobody is allowed any contact, so any socializing has gone bang out of the window. So, time is spent reading, writing, watching the tv or begging to use the telephone. Although a mad day, very quiet in here at the moment, perhaps everyone is chomping on their chocolate or biscuits, which they ordered.

Friday night and here we go again. It's like living with Jekyll & Hyde. Quiet by day and coming to life at night. Shouting, singing and banging. We have a nice quiet time throughout the day and then thunderstorms at night, but the weather is pleasant enough. Batteries are recharged in the day ready for a night of hellish disturbance.

We are heading into Ramadan now at the end of April. Inmates who are participating are being given food packs to see them through the night after fasting throughout the daytime hours. Saturday can be a very long day. Newspaper is a must, it helps keeping up with the gossip, has a good TV magazine and a very good selection of crosswords, puzzles and my old favourite the sudoku. Lunch is usually late morning and then afternoon exercise. Leads us nicely into some kind of sport to watch on the tv, if only we had a remote, but they are like gold dust in here.

Saturday night went off reasonably quiet, then 2am, very early hours of Sunday morning, we were greeted to the sound of our African friend attempting to smash his door down and shouting at the top of his voice "Get up, Get up its Ramadan, Get up, Get up and out of your slumber". If he shouted this once, well, it must have been over one hundred times. The night shift totally ignored this and left him to his own devices. I found all of this very bizarre, from his behaviour to the reaction of the guards. What did they hope to achieve by ignoring this man's attempt to ruin everyone's night's sleep and the same pattern developed over Sunday night/ Monday morning. Surely this couldn't continue through the entire days of Ramadan. He needed some sort of intervention from the mental health team. If that didn't happen you could easily see trouble when he was allowed out to shower. Someone is going to get hurt here if nothing is done.

Monday and the start of a new week. Trouble was, everyone was shattered from a weekend of complete disruption. Nobody had slept, the place was like a grave yard, inmates catching forty winks here and there, to replace those hours lost over the weekend. We had gone from complete madness to silence. Nothing could be heard, apart from the odd jangle of keys, as inmates took their turns to phone loved ones.

As everyone settled down for the evening the silence was broken by our African friend. He went into demolition mode early; it was only 6.30pm. The noise was unreal, how could one man make so much noise I thought. Then this time the sound of many guards running could be heard. Doors slung open and pleasantries exchanged, an eerie silence drowned out the noise of guards dispersing back to their duties. Perhaps he was as shocked as us, that they were ready and waiting for him. It was 7pm and the silence reigned for a couple of hours and then he tried his luck again. The guards must have been waiting and he received exactly the same response. What they did, I will never know, but it did the trick on this occasion. It was as if the guards had taken back control, they appeared to again disperse and return to their duties. Silence, everyone waited with baited breath, but nothing; the night passed away without any further incidents and we all had a good night's sleep.

Tuesday 27th April and we have an early morning visit, at the door we have a guard and another guy, who is from Immigration and they wanted to talk with Tad. Now Tad's English is limited to say the least, almost non-existent would be more accurate. The guard left us with Immigration and they asked if I could help talking with him as we had some sort of understanding already. I was only too pleased to help. This was going to be an education.

It became apparent that Tad had travelled from Vietnam to Calais living rough along the way. They had been transported from Vietnam to Russia by lorry then told to make their own way to Calais. Using any means of transport possible, my understanding was that he had walked, which took several months. Once in Calais he was provided transport in a hidden compartment above a lorry drivers bunk. This cost in the region of £15000.00, the lorry drivers cut being £3000. The money looks like it has been borrowed, which explains his fear of returning home, but this was a distinct possibility. Fingerprints and photos taken he was now on Immigrations hit list. They asked if he wanted to stay in England, of course he did, would you want to return owing money. He had made it; his dream was so much closer, if he could convince them to let him stay in the UK. "Vietnam no good", he kept saying.

Then a whole load of questions, from his home address to his next of kin. Then his date of birth "today 27th April" he said. We knew he was 24 but what we didn't realize was his birthday was today, two days before mine. Its birthday week, very solemn though. Now what were the chances of both our birthdays being in the same week. I ask you?

Back to Immigration and would he be allowed to stay in the UK.

Very unlikely I thought let's look at the facts. He is here as an illegal immigrant, he was caught in a house full of cannabis plants, has nowhere to live, speaks very little English and a pending date in court. Not the best cv to have. So, Immigration left leaving him a timeline as follows;

Monday 3rd May - Appt Immigration
Tuesday 11th May – Appt Solicitor
Monday 17th May – Crown Court

He, or should I say' we; have two weeks to get prepared and at the same time contemplate his fate at the hands of the Crown Court and then Immigration. His favourite line was "Vietnam no good". I tried to explain to him that he needed more than that for his defence. I needed to try and make him understand how precarious his situation was and he should make some notes ready for his solicitor/barrister.

So, Tad's birthday went off much like any other in prison I guess, just another day in here really and mine would probably be no different. How right I was; neither my wife or myself were in the mood to celebrate. Cards came from relatives. I cherished them all, especially hers. We were both on the same wavelength, we could celebrate on my release. Faggots and a glass of orange & pineapple on the menu for me and that was it. Unfortunately, Tad was going downhill fast. His mood was low and he was spending more and more time in bed. He seemed to have the weight of the world on his shoulders, he had no one to turn to, apart from some foreign speaking Arsenal supporter. Life can be tough. I really feel for him at the moment.

CHAPTER SIX – HORIZON

Thursday night and our African friend is in a bad way. I have found out his name is Leroy and judging by the sound of things we could be in for a long eventful night. Every cell has a small window, with Perspex in and a flap on the outside, which the guards like to keep closed in general. Leroy has managed to smash this small window which is about a foot in height by a couple of inches wide and now he is smashing the contents of his cell and throwing out of his new found hole in his door. His TV has been dismantled along with any cupboards that he can smash and make small enough to place though the hole. Eventually with most of the contents of his cell piled up outside of his cell, silence has broken and we all manage to get some sleep.

The following morning, everyone else is going about their normal shower, phone call etc and downstairs the inquest looks to have started, the so-called clipboard brigade had arrived, officers from higher up the food chain. Leroy was still shouting and raising his voice. Did they not have a duty of care to the rest of us inmates. Surely, they could handle and decide what to do with one individual who was on a mission to self-destruct. The inquest continued and the day fell into its usual mad Friday, no exercise, as it was supermarket delivery day.

I was beginning to form relationships with other inmates and the guards who walked our floor every day. I was making mental notes in my head of their names, they were my lifeline, someone to talk to everyday and keep abreast of what was happening inside the prison. I decided to find out how much longer the so-called segregation unit would be directly below us. Pleasant surprise, good news was a foot, the painting was nearly finished and the bad lads would be returned to the basement in the next week. Perhaps then we can settle down and get some sleep on a regular basis. Tad was really happy, he used to hate not being able to sleep at night.

It was generally considered that Friday was one of the worst days of the week here, no exercise, some weeks no showers and today we had an African who had basically lost the plot, being on a mission to cause as much disruption as he possibly could and would. With his cell in ruins, they decided to move him to the cell directly beneath ours, this didn't bode well, I thought. The afternoon passed by quietly, he must be sleeping his late night off. 5.30pm, everyone had just had their evening meal and he started again, this lasted for around 45 minutes then the guards took action and he fell silent. Goodnight, let's hope anyway.

I have learnt quite a bit today; downstairs in one end of the basement is segregation and at the opposite end is what they call the Parsons Suite. Sounds interesting, but this is for the prison workers from the kitchen, laundry etc extra privileges down there, doors left open longer, their own laundry service, sounds like it's just a nicer part of the prison, that's if there is such a thing.

The weekend turned into the Leroy show, another cell ripped apart, furniture flying all over the shop, the language was hotter than the English dictionary could handle and we were getting absolutely no sleep whatsoever. The entire wing was restless, abuse was being fired at Leroy from all angles and yet the guards did nothing. What other inmates had prepared for him was going to be very entertaining if he was ever allowed to mix. Could all of this have been avoided, I'm not sure, it sounded like he was asking to know the days football results, but with no TV and some very annoyed guards, no information was being offered in his direction. In general, it appeared the guards either didn't want to deal with him or didn't know how and the rest of us had to pay the consequences, so be it.

Unfortunately, it was Bank Holiday weekend, Mayday. Outside it would be enjoyed by many in here it was a recipe for disaster. No dancing around maypoles or flag waving for us on the 1st of May. The only good thing was that the weather was more like the middle of winter than a spring day, which didn't really make any difference to any of us. It turned into a very slow, but luckily a quiet day. It turned out that Leroy was from Jamaica, even he had given up the ghost and now we know why. The guards decided to let a couple of the inmates go and have a chat with him, now read into that what you will, like me, use your imagination. I think it was explained in our language how we were missing out on sleep and that it had to stop straight away. It did the trick anyway; silence had again reigned over HMP Leicester.

By the time Wednesday arrived the weather was bitter, it was like the middle of winter and our cell was far from being very warm. The heater, if you could call it that, was like a fluorescent tube about 3 foot in length. It got quite hot but didn't do much. I decided to take myself off to the library, this was downstairs near the kitchen area. There was a librarian and one male guard on duty. Both of whom were quite chatty. Turned out the guard was a Tottenham fan, just what I needed, not. The rule of thumb was the more you got out of your cell, the more people you came into contact with and the days passed faster. I hung around chatting, selected a couple of books, one being Russell Brand- Recovery. Sounds just up my street and it must help in here.

Wednesday afternoon exercise and it's absolutely freezing. This will sort the weak from the chaff I thought. I made it to the yard and there was the grand total of five including me, it was the guys who like to have a walk I think they're from Albania, friendly lads though. The tongue waggers were all tucked up in the warmth of their cells.

Once the evening meal was served and everybody was banged away for the night it was very rare you saw anybody but tonight was different. 6pm and the jangling of keys, our door is open. One of the guards, female and a guy in shirt and trousers carrying a clipboard; very unusual I thought. They asked Tad to wait outside, 'what's coming here' I wondered. They both enquired as to my wellbeing "I'm fine" I said. It turns out the prison had run a poetry competition which I entered; my rendition called Suicidal Stress had won. Trouble was it was so good and so meaningful they were concerned I might kill myself ha-ha. I have passed that moment, they thought it reminded them of the lyrics to the song Bridge Over Troubled Water by Simon & Garfunkel. Compliments indeed. No prize to be seen unfortunately, this was to be delivered later, nice one I thought. They left, went on their merry way having made my night, something to feel proud about for once, and that's been a while.

They did leave me with a copy of the Prison Times and asked me to enter the national competition being run by Koestler arts, this would be a pleaser, but you have to get it signed off by an officer. Nothing to lose, so in for a penny in for a pound.

CHAPTER SEVEN – PROBATION

Rumours were in the air that either today, Thursday, or tomorrow, the segregation wing would be moving back to the basement. I wonder how long it will take them to wreck that. How judgemental can I be?

Young Tad had been complaining about toothache for about a week now and this afternoon he was off to see the dentist. Now it's not very often you have anytime to yourself in here. We had mixed emotions. I was looking forward to the afternoon and he definitely was not, oh dear. 2pm off he trotted guard by his side and I went outside on a nice crisp sunny afternoon for some exercise. Usual culprits standing around talking and the few of us walking as we normally do. When I returned to the wing, I expected to see Tad back from the dentist, no sign of him.

Kettle on, cup of tea. Before I had time to make it there's a knock on the door and in walks a well-dressed chap from Probation. Good news I think, he wants to know if I was prepared to leave the prison early on what they call HDC Home Detention Curfew. I could hardly contain my excitement. I wanted to go now, today but that was not happening. It sounded so simple when he explained it to me, now there we're several forms to be filled in and then they had to be sent to every man and his dog, to be authorised. It reminds me of that program on TV called The Cube, this is how it works we take your sentence in days, half it and half it again. Easy, what do they say on the program "Simplify". All of a sudden in an instance 428 days became 107, not that I'm counting mind. I quickly worked out in my head that 107 days would bring me nicely to Saturday 24th July, as it's a Saturday they have to release me on the Friday. No as its HDC it becomes the Monday, but that is so much better than some time next year in 2022.

This is going to take some digesting. Two ways to look here; positively, or the opposite negatively. First off, I was a little disappointed that I couldn't go today and then I was thinking early July, neither were meant to be. On the other hand, I was ecstatic that I would walk out of here on Monday 26th July into the arms of the most fantastic woman, my wife. Now without her I could never have done this, not in a million years. She could just as easily have walked away and left me to get on with things. I wouldn't have blamed her. But no, we talk every single day about absolutely everything; normally I ring her between 9 & 10 am. She is the love of my life, my best friend, my world and the reason why I will see this through to the very end. I owe her my life and will repay her tenfold, no matter what.

The afternoon progressed and Tad was nowhere to be seen! Where can he be only gone to see the dentist, I thought. Eventually just before the evening meal he returned looking none the worse. This was not going to be easy, he was in no obvious pain, so what happened. It turns out the dentist wants to remove his tooth, but he wanted to discuss it with me first. I'm starting to feel like his dad, why wouldn't you have it removed, it will be cheaper in here than on the outside. So, we had to make another appointment and wait again; great, that wasn't the plan, but there we are.

Not been a bad afternoon and it was about to get even better. My first prize in the poetry competition has arrived. Now I have no hair and what's the first thing out of the goody bag yes, large bottle of shampoo, very funny. Chocolate, cereal bars, crisps, shower gel, soaps, lots of nik naks that will never go begging. Tad was happy anyway.

Friday and its judgement day for segregation, looking down, they all get marched away to their new surroundings one by one. Two guards per inmate, just in case, you never know in here that's for sure. Cleaners move in and all of the cells appear to get a deep clean, it's a well drilled operation and before you know it, they are all occupied again. By teatime the wing is overflowing, it's either been a bad day in court or the induction wing is now empty.

Funnily enough it's very quiet and I think we are in for a good night's sleep, no banging, no shouting I have stayed in much better hotels but all of a sudden what an improvement, let's hope it lasts. As the weekend was upon on us again, I think everyone was trying to catch up with their sleep, last weekend was a nightmare. Outside, the weather had turned to torrential rain and the exercise yard was flooded, looks like a weekend indoors catching up on some reading and writing for me. Saturday afternoon I took a shower, as it was quiet, I took a look in the cleaning cupboard. Oh my god a mirror, now the rule of thumb was if you see something that you want and need, take it. For the first time in a month, I could shave with a mirror, easily pleased me, turning in to quite a weekend.

Then just when you think things can't get any better, we receive fantastic news. Every cell is to be fitted with a telephone. Unbelievable I cannot contain my excitement, being able to ring my wife any time of the day, absolutely amazing. I thought all my Christmas's had come at once. Segregation gone, a mirror and now a telephone everything does come in threes. What a weekend! You imagine how the guards feel; usually they have to get all inmates through the telephones on the landing every day, that must be a logistical nightmare. So, it works both ways.

More good news; Auntie Janice, who worked in the prison service, has told my wife that once my HDC is approved they might get rid of me sooner if they need the space. I could be on the list for an early departure. Finally, Covid restrictions are starting to be lifted and visits could soon be back on the menu. Even the gym is back on the horizon in the next couple of weeks. Everything is finally heading in the right direction, thank heavens.

CHAPTER EIGHT - FIRE

New week arrives. Young Tad has a meeting with his solicitor and a translator is at hand to explain everything to him. Thank heavens for that. All this leading up to his court appearance which is nearly upon us. Communicating with Tad is never easy on a good day. Having established a good relationship with our librarian I popped along to see her this morning, with method in my madness. Couple of new books for me to trudge my way through and to enquire if they had a Vietnamese dictionary. To my delight she did and I could have it for twenty-four hours. Translating to English would allow me to communicate with Tad so much better and after his day, this would be a god send.

He returned from his meeting and was very down. The meeting hadn't quite gone the way he expected. He was still maintaining his innocence though, but when you're found in a house full of cocaine plants, you're on a sticky wicket I suppose. Time will tell. Tad is quiet and although we have the dictionary he takes to his bed, something of a familiar theme over the last week or so. I cannot imagine what is going through his head at the present time. I use the evening to make a note of some useful words in Vietnamese. Phrases which I feel could be helpful to us both over the coming weeks. The dictionary had to be handed back in the morning and it was in my name.

Now with Leroy and the rest of segregation comfortably locked away in the basement, you could be forgiven for thinking everything was going to be a bed of roses over the coming weeks. Today had been a good day, Wednesday. A trip to the library, followed by a cheeky stop off at the pharmacy for a weigh in. Hard to know where you stand with your weight, but I was pleasantly surprised that I was no different to when I arrived, still around 101kg. The nurses said "you will never lose any weight in here", time will tell and we will see. If I continued to eat healthy and carried on my exercise regime there was no telling what I could achieve.

Back to the bed of roses. I haven't forgotten, teatime arrived which went off as usual quite peacefully. In one of the cells opposite ours was an English guy around 30, very dark skinned would be an understatement. He was not in a good frame of mind; next we know he has started to smash everything in his cell. Here we go again. Leroy eat your heart out, this guy was on a mission. Guards turned up and many of them this time. Took a look and left him to it, very strange behaviour from everyone involved really. They obviously thought they had the situation under control, by leaving him to continue in demolition mode. How wrong they were again. I hasten to add, they seemed to be consistent in making very poor judgement calls. Next, we have the fire alarm going off, guards come running from every direction, hoses are pulled from walls as the smell of fire starts filling the wing, he has set his cell on fire. Interesting decision when you have absolutely no way out.

The quick reaction of the guards has seen the fire very quickly extinguished, now we have a further half a dozen guards in full riot gear and the young man is taken away in hand cuffs. Segregation for him and a charge, from the prison, of arson. How to extend your stay at HMP in one easy lesson, silly boy. The smell from the fire was an awful stench and lingered throughout the wing, a dozen or so guards were left to clean up the mess between themselves. Now I understand why each cell has like a two-inch step as you enter, they have seen this happen before. Water then just sits in the cell when the fire has been put out. Clever thinking, me thinks!

I was wondering how an earth anyone could manage to start a fire. To my amazement Tad showed me, lots of the lads are always smoking on their little vape machines. I have never bothered with any of this but if you separate the small cylinder from its base, place a piece of paper over instead and keep clicking eventually this will ignite, simple. Finally, Tad had actually taught me something. They are an arsonist's best friend, it would seem.

Five weeks have passed now since that awful, crushing April day, behind which laid two years of torment, coming to terms with what exactly I had done. The clouds had slowly gathered building to the crashing conclusion. My wife and I used to walk two or three days a week for around an hour; we had different routes around where we lived and I think we both used to wonder about what exactly the consequences would be. We had been fighting with this bombshell for two years. How did we come through those two years having kept it to ourselves for so long? The company involved acted so inappropriately throughout and we should have dealt with their behaviour sooner. There're two sides to every story, they cannot be happy with the way they behaved, to try and bribe my wife was about as low as they managed to get. An awful man who we should have dealt with via the employment laws at the time, maybe there's still time. Let's get out of here first.

Some people might bury their heads, feel sorry for themselves and just give up the ghost. But not me. I am made of stronger stuff; there stands a ladder before me and I sit very firmly right at the bottom of this ladder, having fallen from quite a height, the good news is there is only one way for me to go now and that is upwards. There are opportunities within the prison like working as a mentor for the Shannon Trust, helping other inmates with Maths and English, alike. This could be a useful step back on this ladder as I try to rebuild my life and my wife's for that matter. People Plus work with all the inmates within the Education department. Not sure if I will be here long enough to head down that route though. Then take my young friend Tad, he looks at me as a father figure. I watch his back everywhere we go, he is slight in build, looking like a startled rabbit in the headlights really, he must be so frightened about his future, where he will end up after this mad experience.

When we go our separate ways, I will probably never see him again; sad really.

Now I usually hate Fridays in here, they are just so boring, no exercise and all that, but this Friday we are taking delivery of our in-cell telephones, so exciting. We have been told we will be able to use them immediately, the excitement is just too much. Ringing, talking and being able to communicate with my wife anytime during the day, this is a whole new ball game, low moments, high moments, this is definitely another step on my ladder that I keep talking about, another step small step in the right direction.

Hopefully, the new phones will give the guards much more time on their hands. The logistical nightmare for them is over; perhaps now they will have more time, enabling us showers and exercise. Perhaps even a decent gym rota could be made available. We can only hope at the moment.

This Friday night was very different to any night I had known previously in here, normally the landing lights go off 8/9pm. Not tonight, they stayed on and it sounded like there was a party going on upstairs. All you could hear was that humming noise that you get when you're in a very full pub and everyone is chattering away. Occasionally this was broken, sounding like someone was getting a good hiding, normal Friday night down the pub and this went on until the early hours of the morning. I eventually just dropped off to sleep.

It's a strange place, prison; it plays games with your mind. Every day is another day closer to going home and back to some sort of reality, whatever that may be. Some of the guys seem to think it's always somebody else's fault, the situation that they are in is never down to them and their actions. They're all constantly thinking that the guards are the enemy and having little ongoing wars all the time. Is there really any need? In here you have to take responsibility for your own actions, acknowledge why you are here and as much as you may hate it, you have to embrace your time, learn from it; trust me, there is no other way. The time goes quicker and I personally think it makes you a better person.

CHAPTER NINE- CUP FINAL DAY

Saturday 15th May and it's the cup final Leicester v Chelsea. Now I don't follow either and I don't really care who wins, being an Arsenal fan, I have had plenty of run ins with Chelsea fans over the years and then living in Leicester, well, their fans are no different to any other I suppose, spoilt maybe, over the last few years, but trust me, what goes around comes around and we are all never far away from that slippery slope. 5.15pm kick off; dinner was being served early, so the kitchen staff could watch the game; nice gesture, I thought, just the rest of the day to deal with.

Saturday dinner was the same every week, basically it was like a brunch. Bacon, egg, waffles, sausages and beans, all the usual suspects you would expect on a late breakfast. Today we had at lunchtime, which was quite good for me, as I enjoyed and then wandered off for my afternoon exercise. 4000 steps this afternoon, before we all settled down to watch the game, surely it couldn't be as bad as the semi-final we watched. I had heard how the inmates like to give the doors a good kicking, when a goal was scored in here and was quite looking forward to the noise

Game underway and I was wrong it was actually worse than the semi-final; absolute garbage, no goals, no atmosphere, basically just no fun. All I wanted was for each team to score so I could gauge the reaction when either team managed a goal. I know we are in Leicester but these lads are from all over the world.

Second half and after around 65 minutes finally a goal for Leices-

ter and the place went nuts. Great goal from around thirty yards, which reminded me of the 1971 final when Charlie George scored for Arsenal against Liverpool. Funny I should remember that haha. In fairness the noise made by the inmates was absolutely amazing, credit to them; now I wanted to know how loud it would be if Chelsea managed a goal.

Five minutes left and time was running out. Chelsea score, the noise was thunderous, I thought the place was falling to bits; fantastic, but wait a minute it's gone to VAR, there is a hush across HMP Leicester, you could have heard a pin drop, then offside, the goal is disallowed, this time the Leicester supporters go nuts; doors being thumped, kicked and banged with pots and pans. Amazing few minutes then the final whistle and off we go again, more than I bargained for really, very entertaining.

That was that and by the sound of car horns being blown, lots of shouting and cheering. It sounded like the whole of Leicester was out for a party. A couple of beers would have been very nice right now, everything comes to those that wait, hopefully.

Sunday was like the Lord Mayors show, absolutely throwing it down with rain; the heavens had opened big time. Which is bad news for us, no exercise and a day locked up. Tomorrow was another new week and young Tad was in court, so we were expecting an early morning call. He was struggling through Sunday, the best he could and the only way he knows how, by taking to his bed. Looking at the weather you couldn't really blame him for that. Obviously so much on his mind before his pending date before the judge.

Monday morning and the expected early morning call fails to arrive. Tad could either have to attend court in person or appear via a video link, no early start so I'm guessing that it's going to be the latter. We were both up early, hard to explain to someone who speaks little English. 8am, finally the door opens and we are told that he will be appearing via a video link, leaving him to sit and ponder until around 10.30am. Tad being Tad, decided to take himself back to bed for a while, he always hides under his quilt when the going is too much for him. Easy for me to understand; whether he knew what was going on, really not sure, he was definitely suffering in silence. I was helpless. He was getting more and more unsettled by the minute. It was clear he had been told to say nothing about any of the circumstances which have landed him here and if he did speak out his family would be harmed in some way. He certainly had the weight of the world on his shoulders.

10.30am arrived, no escort for Tad. He was pacing up and down by now. Eventually, his escort arrived at 11.30am, he was a wreck. This gave me some time alone to sit and reflect. Lunch arrived a baguette and supplies for the next twenty-four hours. I wasn't really sure how long Tad would be away, but, 1pm, the door opens and he is back with me. He has deteriorated even further making out to me that he had no solicitor, wasn't able to offer a plea and had to return to court on Friday 28th May. Very strange. I knew the only way I could find out what happened, was to wait for a letter from his solicitor, which would arrive in about five days or so.

Exercise time and Tad had taken to his bed. I decided I actually needed a break and went off to the yard, leaving him some time to himself. It might be what he needs and he can always phone home to speak with his mum during this time. My relationship with the guards was good and I told them he needed some time with the other four lads from Vietnam, who usually came and had a chat when he was really down. This might be a way to finding out what really happened and the best way forward leading up to his next court date.

The guards obviously listened to what I was saying; surely they had a duty of care to him. The four lads from Vietnam shared a bumper cell down on level two and the guards fetched Tad and let him spend the afternoon with his friends, nice touch I thought. It worked; he retuned just before dinner with puzzles, playing cards and generally in a much better frame of mind than before. I thought if he wanted or needed to talk, he would when he was ready, so I just left him to his own devices for now.

I had plenty of issues of my own and had spent the last twenty-four hours trying to help Tad. 6pm, time for a chat with my wife. Oh, the joy of an in-cell telephone and Tad never had a clue what we were talking about, almost private. What a great decision to ring her, now we have been trying to arrange a visit for the last fortnight, first thing she said "have you heard". I was always last to know anything. "They have phoned, I'm coming to see you to-morrow, Tuesday". Amazing I was over the moon and my mood changed in an instant. I was going to see my darling in less than twenty-four hours. What a fantastic way for my day to end.

How an earth was I going to sleep tonight I just couldn't contain my excitement. Thoughts running through my head, everything was new to me, not been to visits before, what would she wear, how would she look, my mind was on fire, roll on Tuesday.

CHAPTER-TEN
THE VISIT

Tuesday morning up very early, sleeping was far from easy. Today, I will see, my wife, for the first time since the 9th April. I had to find something to occupy myself. It was going to be a slow morning, leading up to her visit at 2.10pm. How right I was. It feels like the clock is going backwards and I know when the time arrives, the clock will go into fast forward mode. I went off to exercise for 45 minutes; that would surely help pass some time away. Then, on my return I had delivery of my visiting kit. Nice, striped blue shirt and a pair of jeans, we all had to wear the same.

2pm approaches and this time it's me pacing up and down the cell, clean shaven, nicely dressed and ready for my little trip over to the other side of the prison. This will be the closest I have been to the exit in my entire time here. The guard turns up dead on 2pm and off we go. Out into the sunshine we go past the education block and approach the visits centre. Four visits underway and space for us. Rules are stay seated, two metres apart, no touching in any way shape or form, masks to be kept on at all times (covid), no kissing and on best behaviour at all times. I can just about manage that. Five minutes pass by and I'm starting to worry; is there a problem and they won't let her through security. The mind loves playing games with us. Then in she walks a breath of fresh air, gliding across a darkened sky like a bright new star. Looking absolutely fantastic. I wanted to do all the things which I have just been told that I'm not allowed to, but she was here sitting in front of me.

What was I going to do with all these pent-up emotions, keep them firmly locked away ready for another day; it just wasn't right, but rules are rules and I know they are there to be broken, not this time though? We are both covid free, having received the two vaccinations each, (what is the matter with the people running this prison, madness, you only have to look at all the food waste every day to know something is not quite right.)

Anyway, we sat quietly talking, chatting away and after the slowest of mornings the clock was flying round. It must have been the fastest hour in history. I knew this would happen, that's life for you, spending so much time looking forward to something and it's gone in the blink of an eye. I didn't want her to go. I knew we had to go our separate ways, heart wrenching, so many things I wanted to say and do for that matter. It would all have to wait for a more appropriate moment. My emotions had been shot to pieces. Happy to see my wife, but trudging back to the wing I was a beaten man, a lonely sad figure, downhearted, nowhere to go, perhaps I could do a Tad and take to my bed. Not my style though. I will ring her instead to make sure she got away alright.

Our reunion is going to be a fantastic day, there will be lots of tears, I know for sure, lots of happiness, excitement with overwhelming joy and the sooner the better. The day was moving on ;macaroni cheese for dinner, that should be interesting, no doubt. My young friend Tad ordered the same, his face was a picture, disgusted, by that look; made me smile. Apparently, he doesn't like cheese, bad choice in that case. I thought the clue might have been in the title, funny world.

Yesterday's visit was a real boost, the shot in the arm I needed. Little did I know there was more good news to follow. I have been here in HMP Leicester for nearly six weeks now. Leicester is a remand prison meaning that, as I have been sentenced, I shouldn't be here really. My category is a Cat D prisoner, so I should be in an open Cat D prison. Middle of the morning and I receive a visit from a young lady who is from OMU (Offender Management Unit). Nice young lady and she wants me gone, as I said I shouldn't really be in here. Lots of forms are handed over and I'm told to have them ready to be collected at 2pm. Now I feel quite emotional; could a move be on the cards? I ring my wife to keep her in the loop; we are both quite excited. I spent the hour completing all the forms ready for her return.

Two o'clock arrives and a guard opens up and invites me to the legal department, now never been here before. Numerous locked doors, gates, then some outdoor stairs which lead up to another door. Inside is very legal, different rooms, all which look like they are used for video links to the courts. Very interesting, somewhat intimidating perhaps. The young lady who had brought the forms over earlier was waiting for me, she wanted to fast track me out of the prison and the nearest Cat D prison was Sudbury, about 15 miles away. Not so sure now, that will be a hike for my wife. The meeting lasted about 90 minutes, lots of questions about my suitability for a move.

Sudbury is an open prison; inmates are encouraged to work locally and they run their own garden centre where inmates can work. You're allowed to come and go between certain hours, staying within a certain radius of the prison. So, my wife could come up and we could go for lunch or just a coffee. It sounds very positive stuff, at the moment that is. Everything has a name in prison and a move to Sudbury is no different: ROTL (Release on Temporary license), obvious I thought.

Then we went on to discuss my release on HDC in July. I have plenty of questions, like how long would I have to remain on curfew, which means I have to be home between the hours of 7pm and 7am. Twelve hours in and twelve hours going about your daily day to day life. I also thought I would be on HDC for the entirety of my sentence, but no, I was pleasantly surprised. I would serve 15 weeks in prison and another 15 weeks on HDC, which took me roughly until the 7th November. After we had gone through everything in lots of detail, she was going to get sorted asap and come back within the week. Great, I thought.

First job arriving back on the wing was to phone my wife and give her the news. There might just be a light at the end of the tunnel. The clouds appear to be slowly lifting and hopefully, our next visit, we might just be able to touch, hug and maybe even a kiss, fingers crossed that is.

CHAPTER ELEVEN- MELTDOWN

With the weekend approaching, my young friend Tad has gone in to complete meltdown. I was thinking after his court appearance, that he may settle down for a few weeks, in reality he has spiralled out of control, gone completely in the opposite direction. Nobody is really sure what happened in court and until we receive his letter from his solicitor we are completely in the dark.

He had done his usual trick which was starting to become a little boring and taken to his bed, all morning/afternoon. There was a little bit of hope on the horizon as it was canteen supermarket day, thankful for small mercies. Not today though. Tad lives off noodles, hence he orders about ten packets a week. Today they are out of stock; this isn't going down very well and he takes this as a personal attack. That is Tad for you, back to bed, great! Going to be a long weekend if this continues. You would have thought he had just been told he is being deported in an hours' time, totally off the rails. This will take some pulling back.

During the week, I had been talking with the guards about how low he was and they had placed him on the vulnerable list, luckily. The door opened and the guard was checking on his welfare, obviously he was less communicative than usual, which is saying something. I explained, as usual and off she popped down to see the other guys from Vietnam. They had plenty of noodles and sent him enough to see him through until next week. They were very good like that, helping each other whenever they could. Not a word from Tad. I was angry and told him to say thank you. He just took himself back to his bed and wallowed in self-pity. What was he thinking? Maybe about what laid ahead, or not as the case may be. Strange behaviour, I thought, but then that's just me.

Tad's problems are of his own self making just like everybody else in here. We could all take the easy option and bury our heads in the sand. What use would that be and to whose benefit. I understand a little of where he is coming from unable to communicate for long periods of time, no one to actually talk to or have a meaningful conversation. Then every inmate has their own problems to deal with, as I do, and that's my priority the same as everyone else has theirs. He is like a fish out of water or a rabbit caught in the head-lights, no comprehension of how the system works here and will probably end up on a plane back to Vietnam.

Putting it simply, at the end of the day he is here illegally, was found in a cannabis house, has absolutely no family here, nowhere to live, broken the law and every tax payer will expect him to be dealt with appropriately and sent home. Why should he remain in this country?

I thought to myself that a good night's sleep would sort him out? How wrong I was; he buried his head even deeper in the sand and there was no communication at all. If he doesn't snap out of this somehow, he is in for a lonely ride and lots of sleepless nights. Not much more I can do to help him.

All of which has left me with a very quiet weekend. Writing has become the norm for me I would never have believed it a couple of months ago and to actually start writing poetry, amazing stuff. I have now written fourteen, on various subjects from suicide to our wedding. Two I have entered into Koestler Arts yearly competition, fingers crossed there. Not really interested in the prize; I just want to win and be successful, bit like selling. I want to be the best, number one. What an acclamation that would be, considering I have never written anything before in my life.

Probation have confirmed that my move to Sudbury is imminent and that is where I will spend the second half of my time in prison. Apparently, the paperwork is done and been signed off, just waiting for the knock on the door to say your transport awaits. Could be today, could be tomorrow or maybe even next week, that nobody seems to know. Mixed emotions about moving, what will happen to Tad and who will look out for him. I know he has the lad's downstairs but one of them is due to be deported and another released to Leeds, where he has a wife and child. I suppose they will move him to be with the others downstairs.

In here, communication is very poor on a good day. We are always last to know everything although a couple of the guards don't seem that clued up. Staff turnover appears to be high and they all seem to work in different ways, having different ideas on how the wing should be run. There are no two alike, that's for sure. If our induction is anything to go by, you can imagine that their training probably is just as bad.

Today and the first sign of any real trouble between inmates. Two lads take a dislike to each other and its handbags at ten paces. Fortunately, plenty of guards about and the trouble ends as quick as it began. In hindsight you could imagine if somebody really wanted to cause harm to another inmate, it wouldn't be that difficult. It would be just a matter of biding your time, waiting for that moment and then strike, goodnight, Vienna. Working here can't be an easy job or a nice occupation for that matter. Living your life on tenterhooks, not knowing from one day to the next what is coming; at least I have an end date.

Just about the midway point of my stay here, all being well, that is and on a really positive note, after the Bank Holiday, the last Bank Holiday is in August when I will be at home with my wife. How great is that. I suppose we are now considering whether your glass is half full or half empty. Mine, whatever the circumstances, has always been half full and will always remain that way. Going another step down the line, BBC have started advertising the fact that the Olympics starts in eight weeks, by which time I will be home, just anyway.

Weekend over and today, Tuesday, eventually Tad receives mail from his solicitor. I understand where he is at but I'm not sure Tad quite gets it at the moment. Tad was charged with two other men who are in different prisons. They are claiming they were brought here to be used as slaves and his solicitor is advising him to make the same claim.

When he arrived back from court, he made out he understood nothing apart from the fact that he had to reappear on the 28th June. He seems disappointed that the outcome takes time but he expects an outcome on the 28th. Reading the solicitors letter, he must be wrong. The CPS have until the 28th to submit their evidence and then his legal team have four weeks to respond. Following this he will go to trial first week of December. That's an awful long time to wait; he is down trodden, this is going to be tough for him, if it wasn't anyway.

Quite simple to follow, not when you don't read or write any English though. I explained to him to the best of my ability, not sure if he really understands fully what the implications could well be. He just keeps telling me Vietnam no good, so so sad. True to form, Tad takes to his bed, doesn't respond to anything all night; a long night ahead for him, I think. We will get him some support in the morning, nothing we can do now. Mail arrives late and the night-shift never want to know anything at all. He is just going to have to sleep on it.

If I get shipped out of here, I seriously do feel for my young friend, we have been together since the beginning of this awful ride; in a way, I wish he was going before me. I have no impact on that though, it is what it is.

CHAPTER TWELVE- STAYING PUT

Seven weeks spent here at HMP Leicester and a move firmly on the cards to HMP Sudbury, which is a Cat D prison and it's an open one at that. But just like on "Who wants to be a millionaire", we don't want to give you that. In the blink of an eye, the move is off. All that work with probation, all that time filling out forms and talking over the why and why nots. Along come probation and the move is not happening. No explanation or anything the decision has been made that you will be released from here on Monday 26th July. End of, that's really nice.

We had discussed this. My wife and me only a few days prior. With eight weeks left before my release, we thought they may just leave me alone. I was settled, knew how the prison worked, knew all the staff and the inmates for that matter. Who would gain anything by moving me, even if it was to an open prison? Nobody, was probably the answer and does anybody really like change; No is the correct answer, we are all creatures of habit.

With the Bank Holiday approaching, Whitsun half term week for the schools. I came up with what I thought was a really good idea. Everywhere in here was closed down for three days and the library was always closed on Fridays. So, I popped along to see the Librarian and asked to borrow the Vietnamese dictionary, knowing full well I would have to keep until Tuesday, usually dictionaries were only allowed out overnight. My plan worked and now Tad, who was in quite a good place at present, could read and communicate with me over the weekend. You never know, he might even learn some English. This will give him time to convert his solicitors' letters into his own language and hopefully understand exactly what the situation is; for him to say it has been an education is an understatement, what exactly would he have done without my help, because the prison certainly hasn't helped. I thought they had a duty of care; how wrong I was.

Over the Bank Holiday weekend, you can guarantee everything will stop in here, tools will be put down, nothing will happen from Friday lunchtime until Tuesday lunchtime. It's like going back in time, this small world is saying goodnight for a few days. But the inmates are still here sort of looking after themselves really. We still need food and exercise at the very least. The powers that be talk about re-offending, well it's hardly surprising as this is no deterrent, banging everyone away for twenty-three hours a day; what use is that. They have no understanding of what the problems really are, from Boris so called Johnson as prime minister, his merry men, the judges/judicial system and the people running these very inadequate prisons. The thought of them actually talking to each other about the real problems beggar's belief. Cage people up like animals appears their answer, well don't be surprised when that's how they behave, you only have yourselves to blame.

This country is a mess and some of the people living in it need to have a good look at themselves, instead of trying to line their own pockets, a dodgy deal here and there, thinking about themselves and nobody else. Until society accepts that the powers that be have made a right mess of the system and the system is dead, offenders will keep doing just that. Release them into the wild and they will behave like the wild animals they have come accustomed to being.

New month, June is here, most definitely half way through now, counting down the days. You would think that everyone would be nicely chilled after the long weekend. Not really, everyone has been locked away all weekend and some lads have had a lot of time to sit and stew. The mayhem begins and a lad receives a side swipe, hitting the deck. Guards come running as usual and the lad who was on the receiving end now wants to have a go back, strange that, now the guards are between him and his aggressor. One lad is returned to his cell and the other taken away in handcuffs, probably to see the governor and spend some time down in segregation. How many days, who knows?

Surely that is enough excitement for one day, then maybe not. The landings are cleared, everyone back to their cells, even the landing cleaners are locked away. Guards gather in numbers, riot gear at the ready and when your little windows are covered you know something's about to go off. Lots of noise, shouting, banging, followed by silence. Downstairs they have a cleaner called Woody, he has been found with Black Mamba, some sort of drug to the uneducated like me. Now he decides to barricade himself in his cell, thinking as the doors opened inwards that the guards would struggle to get to him, he was wrong. If you release the latches on the outside the door then opens outwards, what a stupid idea that was. In go the riot guys, four of them we hear, he will be forced back down the cell, put in to cuffs and taken down to segregation. We all know how the system works in here and his job is history.

Recently I have been lucky enough to have done some work with the young lady from the Careers department; yes, they do have such a department, trust me. We get on very well and she has talked to me about my ideas upon my release. Both being massive Arsenal fans probably helps, although she wouldn't remember all the success in the Wenger years during the 90's, far too young.

Her input and visits are vital. When I leave here, I want my own consulting/counselling business. At present she is my link with the outside world. Together we have been in communication with a company called Rift Social Enterprise, who offer inmates twelve months support when leaving prison with things like setting up a website, support in general with marketing, stationary, legal help and much more. I have qualifications in counselling, CBT, nutrition and as a Personal Trainer. If I could add, say, something like meditation or yoga, or even both, this could just work

Addictions is obviously very close to my heart. At the end of the day the gambling is what has destroyed my life and ended me up in here. If we could put a plan together, approach the Education Department at Westminster, then we might just achieve something here. One thing I have learnt over the past few weeks is, if you want something enough, believe in yourself, then you might just make it happen.

CHAPTER THIRTEEN-
BEHAVIOUR

Sometimes you wonder about the mentality of the inmates, what could possibly make them respond in the manner which is obviously going to have a negative impact on their stay in HMP Leicester, or even worse could extend their stay. Their thought pattern could well cause them to lose all privileges and what is the point in that; you need something in here to keep your sanity, whether it's just your television or a bag of goodies on a Friday afternoon for the weekend.

It's a very quiet sunny Thursday afternoon at the beginning of June. The layout of the prison is quite simple. Ground floor houses the twos, first floor is where we are based, the threes and upstairs on the second floor are the fours, how easy is that. Every floor takes exercise at different times throughout the day; this afternoon at 3.30pm, total chaos breaks out. The fours are returning from their afternoon sabbatical when around ten lads make a rush on the staircase leading down to segregation. Lots of pushing, shoving and handbags in general. Guards appear from every direction, in the main everyone is ushered back to their cells and a couple taken straight into segregation. See what I mean about the mentality, hard to fathom really; all a status thing, I guess.

Dinner time approached, but something was brewing upstairs, we all knew someone would pay for this afternoon's disturbance, lots of banging, shouting and screaming was to be heard. The guards were gathering, by now they knew who was responsible for the disturbance and were about to take their revenge. They took out whoever they wanted to really and silence again reigned down over HMP. Dinner was now being served and the guards had definitely had enough, only a few allowed down at a time, never seen this happen before.

The guards seemed to be on a mission taking out inmates who have obviously been on their hit list for some time. Paddy, our floor cleaner, was having his cell searched by a good half a dozen guards and was promptly removed down to segregation. More guards and medics are with an Asian lad who is grossly overweight, code red was called but he remained. They call different colours for different scenarios. To finish off the day, Leroy, who had returned to the wing from segregation, started shouting, only to receive a torrent of abuse from the rest of the inmates. What was going to happen to his parents was shocking; they were giving him everything. Behave Leroy, or who knows what will happen when he comes down for his dinner?

Friday, the day everyone hates, no exercise being the main reason. It has taken on a different mantle for me this week. I told my wife when she came on her next visit to make sure it was a Friday, this would be the perfect remedy to the Friday lock up and she has managed to achieve just that, the highlight of my month, no doubt. At present, we are allowed only one visit per month, but there is talk of that changing to two. We are allowed one hour only and still no form of contact, but it will be great to see her. The usual search on the way into the visit area and our hour began. The room was quiet, we had to sit the regulatory two metres apart and there was lots of chatter going on, everyone just like us, trying to catch up on all of the news. The solitary hour disappears as quickly as it arrived and its time again to say our goodbyes, heart wrenching, hardest thing to do, say goodbye to the person you love most in the world. Great to see her, gives me the boost to make it through the month.

First weekend in June and that means in the sporting world that it's the Derby at Epsom. We have the Olympics only six weeks away and the football Euros begins this week, a year late because of Covid. So, there's a few things to look forward to watching, this month. England, who usually offer so much and produce so little, in most major championships, have half a chance, but there will be lots of other teams thinking very much the same. Bit like my mental health really, well, in recent months anyway. Prepare for the worst, expect absolutely nothing and just hope to be surprised.

We have had quite a quiet weekend, bit like the lull before the storm; everyone has been nicely going about their own business, that makes a pleasant change. Today Monday and I'm thinking that in seven weeks I will be leaving this god forsaken hole and that is really being polite. If I had to think of one word to sum-up this experience, it would be "Education", because it's certainly been that.

Earlier I talked about the constant arguments between Leroy and his friend in the cell opposite, their constant exchange of foul-mouthed obscenities was disgusting on a good day. It needed to be heard to be believed, both of whom ended up down the segregation block, surprise. Leroy was a very deep individual and had some severe issues, whereas the other guy didn't seem too bad and was released last week. To my amazement, he is already back. I was checking out the exercise yard, behind our cell for the new inmates and there he is, as bold as brass. The question I ask myself is why? Why would you risk the chance of ending up back here full stop and one week later at that? There are no words really, but I suppose Leroy will be happy.

Anyway, with seven weeks remaining, the young lady from the Careers department is on the prowl and I appear to be on her radar. The Education department requires someone to do some painting. I knew I should never have mentioned that I was a dab hand with a paint brush, stupid boy. I wasn't thinking of working in here for one moment, but she seems very keen. "Fill this form out, the meeting is tomorrow" she handed me a form, bit like the real world this. I handed her the completed form. "Your application will be heard at the meeting and you have the job" she said. Talk about being fast tracked through the system, she should be in charge of us all being released. Bobs your uncle. Just like that I had a job and that is no mean feat in here, they are like gold dust or as one of the guards said "rocking horse shit".

Then she moves on to RIFT, and the application process for the twelve months support when released. She sends an email; they send a document to me to be completed and we take it from there; good luck to me. To be honest, it has been a really productive day. The gym has reopened and its more by luck than chance. I think, but I managed an hour in there with Tad today. Small little gym, the usual bikes, rowing machines, treadmills, weights and resistance weights, more than enough to keep me happy. Got my 6000 steps in on the treadmill and some weights for good measure. The best time for the gym is 9am when some of the more troubled inmates have not managed to rise from their beds yet. They just don't have the structure in life or motivation to get up that early. I have though and the early bird catches the worm does he not.

One thing you have to do in here is always watch your back, you never know what is coming. Don't turn your back on anyone. Afternoon medication is being given when a very large African guy launches an attack on some unsuspecting lad. More of a brawl this time, the African guy is led away with a rye grin on his face and the other lad is helped back to his cell, looking a little worse for wear. Just another day in here, it wouldn't be the same without a little altercation, now, would it.

CHAPTER FOURTEEN
- SUCCESS

Another week in the asylum, pretty much sums this place up at the moment. How do lads manage to survive in a place like, this when they have a long stretch to look forward to, it's hard to fathom in reality? Both mentally and physically I struggle to get my head around the monotony of the place; another day, another week, they all just continue as one, its beyond my thought process. Finding out that some lads are looking at ten years or more, it makes my sentence and time here feel very different. You form relationships in here with lots of different people from such diverse backgrounds. There's a young lad a couple of cells down, who is up in court for sentencing this week; not quite sure what he is here for, but by the sound of things, he likes using his fists and the odd weapon thrown in for good measure. You just know he has a couple of years locked up to look forward to, what a waste. You try to understand how and why? Has society failed him, but looking at his background you can see a pattern emerging; what went wrong though? He is a nice enough lad, he has never had a cross word with me; every time we meet, he offers the customary fist pump.

Knowing today the young lad is appearing in court, you can only wonder and ponder his fate. I think he knew he was facing time inside, possibly 12/18 months. Around about 4pm I notice that he is back on the wing. Some guards are good, some not quite so, luckily this afternoon its possibly the best guard on duty and he tells me the news "three years" he said. I'm actually stunned.

I never expected that. My first thoughts are for the young man, wanting to know if he was ok. The guards seemed to be talking with him and making sure he wasn't taking the news too badly. To his credit, he seemed fairly calm and relaxed, whereas he could have gone in totally the opposite direction. If he behaves himself and I mean just that he is looking at eighteen months. I could not cope in here for that long.

Meanwhile, my world is still on the up and up. The Education Department have been running another poetry competition and yes, I have won again, very pleased with that little outcome. Almost feel a bit guilty after the news from earlier. Every little victory is a step in the right direction for me and I was milking the moment with the young lady from the Careers department. Two competitions and two victories for me. The prize is the same as previously; a goodie bag, shower gel(handy), drinks, biscuits and chocolate, very nice, thank you.

The good news keeps on coming this week; having been sort of fast tracked down the employment route. There is me having a quiet sort of day and here is my careers young lady again, "get your coat time for work." (Nobody had a coat) Hang on a minute, what's happening here? I was now officially the Education Departments Orderly, what a mouthful. In English means they want some painting doing and I get paid, well sort of anyway. Nine sessions a week Monday to Thursday am and pm, then only Friday am, half day and I get the grand sum of one pound per session, WOW!!!!!

Now, you could be forgiven for thinking that is slave labour and yes, you would be right, but rules are rules. This small amount would help pay for my telephone each week when I speak to my wife. There is method in my madness, secondly it is time out of the cell and away from the wing, clever I hear you say. Now the staff in the Education department are very aware that I only have around six weeks left and there is much to do. It appears that I will be left to my own devices, they all trust me enough to just get on with the job in hand, this is a result. There are a couple of negatives that I will not get into the gym, exercise is totally different for those who work and no library as it will always be closed on my return, never mind.

Whilst I have been in here reading has become a passion. I have tried to embrace my time and to take on board absolutely everything that has happened. I came across one quote about giving, it said "the more we give, the more we receive back, in fact tenfold". This appears to be true, my outlook on life has changed and I have been doing more for people; which will continue upon my release.

Approximately fifteen weeks to spend in here and here we are, week ten and I find myself now in some form of employment, if you can call it that. Escorted over to the Education block and I receive the official tour, two floors and it all needs painting, this could be tight to actually get the whole lot finished by the time I leave, but it's a new challenge and will certainly keep me busy.

Lots of introductions from the boss, teachers and the girls in the office. I will never remember all of their names. The boss has a rough idea of what she would like doing, so we set out a plan for the coming weeks. Breaking it all down to a week at a time. The offices were very drab and needed brightening up, as did most of the classrooms and the corridors. On closer inspection it doesn't look great and the last inmate to have a crack at this must have been closely related to Stevie Wonder ha-ha. I worked it out that by the time I had actually made it over to the department, then returned back to the wing for lunch, doing the same procedure in the afternoon, it would probably leave me around 4 hours painting a day. For a man of my experience, it should be a breeze.

Back on the wing my regime had changed completely. I could join the exercise group in the morning at 8am. I could catch up with a friend who already had a job in the kitchen, now when I say friend, he was actually my wife's Godson, her best friend's son. I could shower very early, which I quite enjoyed, everyone else was still locked away, tucked up in their beds and I was up and about.

Normally the exercise yard could be quite busy with around thirty odd inmates either walking or as normally happens, chatting to each other. This can be quite an intimidating place for the faint hearted. Huddles of young men ranging from eighteen to sixty years old. Most of whom are in here waiting to appear in court, remember this is a remand prison and with the current covid situation playing havoc in every walk of life, the judicial system is floundering, on its knees, almost shot to pieces. One lad told me he could end up serving more time on remand than what his actual sentence might be. Then he's entitled to claim compensation, anything up to one hundred pounds a day, how much is that costing the tax payer I wonder?

But I was no longer on the general exercise routine, apart from weekends. My first jaunt and it's quite different, all of these lads actually have jobs, inside. There was between ten and twenty guys. All still doing the same as the general exercise group, some walking, some talking and a few doing weights.

With my friend on the early exercise, we walked and talked, no stopping us we can multi task, us men, at times anyway. We were quickly joined by a couple of other lads who knew my friend. They asked if I was ok, he put their minds at rest and we carried on walking. These guys could only be described as serial offenders, they knew the system inside out, why wouldn't they, they have jobs of course. Their knowledge of the judicial system was amazing. I was shocked. What they didn't know wasn't worth knowing.

One of the lads who I had exchanged pleasantries with on the wing, was talking about what his sentence might turn out to be. I was all ears. I never knew any of this, it was a complete education for me, yet again. It was second nature to all of them, it followed in this order, well you could get murder being the worst, or attempted murder or a section eighteen with intent or just a section eighteen. Lovely, I was seriously out of my depth here, but because I knew one of the lads, I was accepted into the group for the morning walk and fist pumps were offered whenever any of us bumped into each other on the wing or elsewhere.

CHAPTER FIFTEEN – GOODBYE MY FRIEND

I have spent the whole week over at the Education department. Most of the classrooms needed some TLC and now look much more like what you would expect. Lots of expensive computers, printers, large TV screens and the place had been let go. Now I was on the case it was starting to look as you would expect, for a place of learning. The main office had to be painted by the prisons contractors this weekend. As it was a working office, it had to be painted when all of the systems were closed down. All I had to do was get it prepared and for this the Education department has recruited a cleaner stroke general dogs' body. This was good for me as he was on the same page as me. Although slightly eccentric and as mad as they come.

My little friend from Vietnam however was not in a good place and it took me a while to understand why. He was very quiet, not talking and as usual taking to his bed. The penny dropped. I was working and spending all day out of the cell, away from the wing and he was not coping. I had to do something and spoke with the guards about getting him out of the cell and into the gym on a daily basis. This had the desired effect. All of a sudden, he changed, like flicking a switch he was back to his old self, back on the straight and narrow if there is such a thing in here.

Meanwhile, Leroy was back on the wing yet again, after another spell in segregation and he was hell bent on keeping the entire wing awake, complete madness had broken out. Then Thursday, during the night, he smashed his new cell up, should I say again!

Well, that was the end of that and back off to segregation, he must like it down there.

Each floor has a designated cleaner and painter, for that matter. Our cleaner was keeping his head down, waiting for his court appearance and our painter always looked under the influence of something. I wouldn't want him painting anything of mine. When the going gets tough the guards call code blue or code red. Our painter decided to cut himself badly and the shout was blue or was it red? Red I think, anyway, guards and medics appear from nowhere, lots of blood all over the shop, pouring from his wrists. He has always looked like an accident waiting to happen, he seems to have no concept of reality, hangs about with lads who he thinks make him look big and this was always on the cards.

Meanwhile, the lad who is waiting to find out what charge he is facing; murder, attempted murder or section eighteen, is given a new cell mate, a young lad from Birmingham and before we know it, they have taken a dislike to each other and beat the living daylights out of each other, that was a match made in heaven.

Everything comes in threes and the lad in the next cell has not paid his dues. That's never a good idea in here and he gets a slap on the landing for his trouble. Code blue, he has lost consciousness and is out cold. Guards and medics from all corners, yet again. He comes round and quite quickly he is back on his feet with a beautiful black eye. The way things are in here though, he said he fell and it was his own fault. Of course, nobody saw anything, that's the way it is.

Back to some form of normality, if there is such a thing in here. Before you're allowed to work you have to complete the manual handling worksheets. Very simple, I'm sure a child could have passed. To my delight I passed with 100% and receive a nice certificate to say so. Something to add to my collection. I will take that every day and the picture I am painting is slowly coming together.

My young lady from Careers is on the wing looking for me, she has emailed RIFT and they are very interested in talking with me. More good news. I have always believed that everything happens for a reason; that's probably the best and only way for me to look at this experience. If I walk away from this with a new business venture, then my time has been proactive after all.

This place looks very different now to when I first arrived; we are well into June now and those first images are starting to seem like a dim and distant past, thank heavens. Downstairs the twos have become virtually empty, whilst the builders re vamp the entire floor. Some nights they work until around 9pm, banging and drilling away, not sure what they're actually doing and I won't be hanging around to see the final outcome. Speed does definitely not seem to be one of their strong points.

On our wing the threes, it's like musical chairs but in this case its musical cells, everyone is swapping which cell they are in, as others come and go. Some actually do get released and others get moved after sentencing, to other prisons. Young Tad has started learning English again, thanks to me. I bumped into the English tutor, nice young lady from Germany or something like. Typical, a foreign girl teaching English, that just about sums everything up. He has received several test papers I suppose they are evaluating exactly how good, or in his case, how bad, his English really is.

Meanwhile I have become the darling of the Education department. Whatever or wherever I work I always give it my best shot and the staff all seem to appreciate what I have been doing, bringing the department firmly into the 21st century. In a way it's like being reintroduced back in to the real world. I'm usually left to my own devices and I work to my own goals, knowing exactly where I need to be every day if I'm going to get this job finished before I leave. The staff are friendly and always stop for a catch up, a couple of the teachers you have to avoid or you could spend your entire time listening to them trying to put the worlds to right.

They know who they are!

The manager of the department has certainly made an impact and she has me hanging signs and helping with some art work which she wants hanging. All this, when I have a spare five minutes away from my paint brush. I think I'm becoming more artistic and creative, like a good red wine I'm maturing with age, although my wife might say different. Also, today the unthinkable happened and I was given great trust by the staff. I was allowed to have the scissors and the staple gun, such small things that mean so much.

Inmates change like the wind in here. I have got to know quite a few now and I think I have the general respect of the wing. Who would argue with a well-built 6ft wide juggernaut, well that's how I look at the moment? Built like a rugby player, that's me. When I think about the lads who have moved on, there we're the Albanians, who have been transferred now up to Manchester prison to be closer to family. The young lad, who was sentenced last week, has now been moved to Ranby prison and my early morning walk friend could well be released next week, all being well.

Then there's my young cell mate Tad, from Vietnam. Friday is normally such a boring day and today, just after lunch, the guards arrive to take him to a court hearing via video link, neither of us knew this was happening today. He had only been gone for about an hour, when the door opens and he is back. He is ecstatic "I told you I was innocent, I told you," He said. I couldn't believe what I was hearing, "it's true," said the guard. The court have dropped all charges against him. He now just needs to wait until Immigration have sorted out what they need to do. I don't know who is more shocked, him or me. I'm absolutely speechless.

All this time he has told me he was innocent and I really thought he was spinning me a yarn. The question is, what happens now? The answer to that question; we hadn't got a clue, but if Immigration didn't want him, surely, he was free to go. The afternoon passed we took our usual Friday afternoon delivery of goodies, which would see us through the next week, and then dinner. It was quite a hot summers day and we were all offered iced lollies to go with our dinners, such excitement. As Tad went to start our door opened and two guards stood in front of us, unusual for a Friday teatime. "Come on Tad you're free to go, get your stuff together and we will be back in ten minutes" they said. Both of our faces dropped; what has just happened. He gathered his stuff, one bag of his belongings to take away and another bag full of noodles to give to his friends from Vietnam on the way out.

This was tough, he had been like a son all the time we had been here and, in an instance, he was gone. We said our farewells, he thanked me for looking after him and we wished each other well. The guards wanted to get a move on and before we knew it the door was banged shut and I, for the first time in ten weeks, was all alone. I have no idea where he is going. I shouted at the guards. I wanted to know if he was being released or taken by Immigration? She said "he was being released and they had somewhere for him to stay", that is a relief.

I phoned my wife; the words wouldn't come out; she thought something awful had happened. It was the opposite my little friend had gone and I was full of mixed emotions. I had grown to like the little fellow and I was happy that he was free, but a little scared for him on the outside. At least he has gone before me and I don't have to worry about leaving him in this place. I will miss him, probably never to be seen again. I wish him well and hope only good things for him. I hope life will be kind to him. Good luck my little Vietnamese friend, may God be with you.

This leaves me all alone for the weekend. Not a chance of a new cell mate until next week at the earliest. The Euros has started and everyone is busy watching the football. So now I have seen, whilst in here the world snooker championships, the derby, the cup final, the French open tennis and next, after the Euros, we have the tennis from Wimbledon to look forward to. The final of the Euros and Wimbledon are both on the same day Sunday 11th July by which time I will only have two weeks to go.

Unfortunately, after his five days back down Segregation, Leroy is back on the wing, just when I was looking forward to a nice quiet weekend; some exercise, the paper, some sport and a bit of telephone time with my wife. However, Leroy has a very quiet weekend and we all are more than thankful for that.

CHAPTER SIXTEEN
– PRAISE

New week begins and new challenges to face. Everyone was in a half decent mood after England's victory over Germany in the Euros. Onwards and upwards was the way forward. I knew it wouldn't be long before I was backed into a corner over a new cell mate. I was working in the Education department when one of the guards from the induction wing came heading in my direction. This could only mean one thing, I was faced with the same predicament as I was several weeks earlier, take a new cell mate or I can book you in to see the governor. Now I wouldn't mind a chat with the governor about various different things but not this subject. I gave in, was offered a couple of options and made my choice. He would be with me later today, great!

My early morning walking friend was in court today. I managed to catch up with him and wished him well. Fifty, fifty really as to him being released and the only way to find out his outcome was to clock him on the wing later or to phone my wife. I knew he would contact her if he was released, living just around the corner from our home. Time would tell!

Morning employment finished and we head back to the wing, by which time my new cell mate was beginning to move in. As it happens the induction staff asked the lad opposite me if he wanted to share with me and vice versa. We both agreed, we had seen each other out in the yard and he seemed ok but you never really know. His name was Bob and by moving someone from the wing meant that the guards had a free cell to move a couple down from induction, method in their madness, I guess.

We had a chat over lunch. Bob was in his middle forties and had been given the run around in here. He had been moved all over the place, this can happen in here unless you stick up for yourself and don't take any rubbish from the guards, the system or fellow inmates. I had to get back to my day job, painting was waiting over at Education. They say first impressions are usually the right ones and something was not quite right with Bob, he seemed right enough but it was going to take some time to work out what it was about him. I had enough time, that was for sure.

The afternoon passed and I caught up with the lads in the kitchen at dinner time. They were of the opinion that my friend had been released at court, with the charges being dropped. That was great news, if true. I had told him to stay positive for the last few weeks and if the news was correct, it may have just paid off. I would ring my wife later for confirmation.

Bob was settling in on the top bunk and beginning to open up to me. He had been in and out of prison for many years and this time he was up on a murder charge by the sound of things. My thoughts were, it could have been worse, he seemed just about alright and I could have been placed in a position where I had been sitting opposite a complete nut case. One thing, he was completely different to my little friend from Vietnam.

Middle of the evening and I decided to phone my wife. She said "I have somebody here, who says hello", confirmation my friend had been released and had popped in to let her know the good news. What a result, earlier today he was locked away in here and there he was having a coffee with My wife and his five-year-old daughter as well. He was just waiting for my call before he left. She reckoned he thought I was a top bloke, as did all the other lads on the wing. I try my best. She told me she was proud of the way I had behaved and handled a very difficult situation very well. I hate praise, this I just can't handle. I love her so, so much and she didn't deserve any of this and I definitely don't deserve any shape or form of praise. This is something I have to deal with in the coming months, somehow!

Feeling a bit lonely in here now, my little Vietnamese friend seems long gone and my other friend has now been released, going to be a long three weeks, the time which I have left now. The painting jobs are mounting up in here now, much left to do in the Education department and one of the guards on the wing is developing a small unit, which is to be a barbers, for the inmates. He has heard that I can paint and would like me to do the job before I leave, this is getting out of hand. When did they expect me to paint this little barber's shop? Over a weekend was being suggested, at least that gets me out of the cell every day of the week, I suppose.

Amazingly, Leroy has settled down on the wing now. He has the odd moment, but compared to some of his antics, he is virtually a pussycat at the moment. He appeared in court last week, perhaps he has some goals to aim for now and wants to see the back of this place. One of the guards told me he had taken to writing letters and had last week written to the local cockroach society. Speechless that anyone would consider such an option and further more did we have such a local organization. Heard it all now. He has even been allowed out at dinner time to collect his own dinner; that was a distant possibility a few weeks ago for the fear of another inmate having a swipe at him, how times are changing.

More good news this week. RIFT, who offer the twelve-month business support to inmates released back into society, have agreed to welcome me onto the scheme. This means I get my own business support manager, who will advise me on all different aspects of business, help wherever needed with my website design, solicitors, taxes, printing and much, much more. All the preliminaries are done, just a matter of arranging our first meeting upon my release now.

My young lady from the Careers department has been such great support whilst I have been in here. I would never have made it this far without her. I really can't thank her enough, she has been with me all the way and helped drive me into starting up the business, along with my wife, for whom there are absolutely no words to even start to think how amazing she has been. I'm all ready for my release, letters are written ready to send to many different places, local companies, NHS, Gambling support groups and the Government, who are currently reviewing the gambling laws in this country

Once again, the highlight of my week is this Friday, when my wife, has another visit. The morning always seems to drag and take forever. The one hour when we sit together, talking, always seems to disappear in an instant. It's great to see her, she looks amazing, good enough to eat, but the old covid rules are still in place, no touching or anything like that and we must sit the usual two metres apart, great.

Apart from the odd skirmish, in general, everywhere is pretty quiet at the moment, could be the lull before the storm, who knows? The new barbers is directly opposite the twenty-four-hour seven day a week isolation cell, lovely place. This is currently occupied by our old painter from the threes. He is still on twenty-four-hour watch after self-harming. I was painting this morning and it looks like a horrible place to be incarcerated, no privacy whatsoever, the guards sit watching constantly all day, you couldn't even use the toilet in peace, disgusting state of affairs to find yourself in.

I have come a long way in the time I have spent here; speaking with the offender manager unit today, they told me that I have lots of positive remarks on my file and I should be very proud about this. Here we go again I don't do praise. Officers and staff from the Education department had all placed good remarks about the way

I have behaved, helped others and my general conduct. Seemed the best way to deal with the situation to me, to be honest. One guard even said to me "If everyone was like me and behaved the way I did, he would enjoy coming to work". Nice bloke, one of the better guards, of which there are a few. Soon I will be on my way and by the sound of things, one of the prisons success stories.

CHAPTER SEVENTEEN – SUPPORT

Into July now and my arrival here in April seems like a lifetime ago; how my entire outlook on life has changed in such a short period of time. A positive mindset has now taken over and from being a completely broken man on the edge of taking his own life, here stands this new man before us today ready to take on the world, slowly though.

I have seen many things over the last few months, come across lots of different people from inmates, to guards and all of the staff in the Education/Careers departments. It has certainly been an Education for me in here. I suppose that is the only way I can sum up this experience and to anyone who may follow in my footsteps, good luck to you and the best piece of advice I could give anyone is to embrace your situation, remember you're here down to the decisions that you made and if you fight the system, it could feel that you're here, longer than your actual sentence length.

Going back to our friend Leroy, I thought he had settled down; totally wrong again. He has spent the last three nights making as much noise as he possibly could, shouting and banging his window. The guards will only take so much and now he finds himself back down the basement in segregation. There is just no rhyme or reason with the guy, total madness. One saying I hear, in here, every day is "he is wired wrong". This is said about lots of guys and lots of inmates firmly believe this, have a look in the mirror guys?

Then there is my new cell mate, he has been here on remand

since January, why have you done absolutely nothing to help your-self. Tad was different, he spoke no English. I have chased mental health for him, they just come along and push forms under the door. What use is this? The form is all about PTSD Post Traumatic Stress Disorder, this is good but the guy is dyslexic and has no idea what he is doing, what to write or answer. If anything is wired wrong, it's the system and the prison; he can only use the skills he has available to him, limited at best. The system is definitely fail-ing him.

He has been here six months with no help, we also now have him enrolled in the Education system, which he needs to take the blame for; the old syndrome comes to mind, if you don't ask, you don't get. I wonder how many guys are just sitting in here waiting for somebody to come and knock on the door?

Who would have thought with only two weeks remaining in here, everyone would want a piece of Nick to come and do some paint-ing? The Education department is coming on nicely; classrooms are all finished now, one office is left needing to be painted, as are a couple of corridors. If anything has to be left it will be the corri-dors. I can only do so much. Meanwhile, on the wing the barbers is coming along nicely and will soon be finished.

The Euros and Wimbledon have both reached their respective completions. Bob behaved like a complete idiot during the final of the Euros, cheering on the Italians, definitely something wrong with him. The Olympics is being advertised all over the BBC, with the build up to the opening ceremony, but I don't really think any-body cares that much. It all starts on the 23rd July, four days later I will be on my way home.

One person I wasn't expecting to see was the Priest. Apparently, they always have to see anyone who is about to be released back into the real world. He is a nice chap, always quite chatty, remind-ing me of our local priest in the village at home, could have been twins almost. He wanted to know I was alright and had somewhere to live on my release. The offender management unit were all over me regarding my HDC conditions, what time I would be allowed out, when the tag would be fitted, who would be there, basically a million and one things going on. The prison has started giving inmates one to one sessions again, bit late for me now and all inmates have been allocated an officer to talk to if required. All down to covid restrictions being lifted.

I had a timetable being set for me. Released Monday 26th July early morning. Appointment with probation at 11am in the city centre and then the HDC team will arrive before midnight to set the tag system up, what that entails, who knows? Then, on the Tuesday I have an appointment with the National Careers Department via telephone. More importantly my wife had booked two weeks off work. She was all the support I needed in the first instant; the rest would have to wait a while.

It's Tuesday 13th July and all has been quite subdued for a while now, even Leroy is behaving. Perhaps with it being the 13th something had to happen. 6pm and our local fire starter, who was back on the wing, decided to fire his cell again. He decided we all needed some entertainment, completely smashed up his cell before setting it alight. This lad has now fired up four cells on different occasions. Bells are ringing everywhere, guards scuttling about, fire hoses being dragged from walls; the acrid smell of smoke and finally the sound of the fire brigade arriving on site.

Usually, the guards enter quickly and remove the occupant; this time, they seemed to take longer and by the time two guards with all the protective gear enter and remove the guy, he looks in a bad way. He is sweating profusely but still cuffed and taken away, idiot! He is, by now obviously suffering with smoke inhalation and the guards put an ambulance on stand-by. The fire brigade must love coming to this place, they arrive spending time in making sure the fire is extinguished before some sort of calm follows. The smell of burning wood and plastic is awful, the air is full of it and leaves a bad taste in the mouth.

With the fire now under control and the guards starting to re-group. They must have decided they had had enough and consequently started searching all of the cells close to the vicinity of the fire. The fire was in sixteen, they went into eighteen which was occupied by a couple of very dodgy looking characters, they removed some tablets, good start, they then entered fourteen with exactly the same result, both lads removed, cuffed and taken straight down to segregation. The dodgy chaps in eighteen appeared to be left to stew overnight, apparently segregation was now full, luckily for them. That was that, the guards looked shattered; some had started their shifts at 7am this morning and now it was 9pm. No doubt some would be back on shift early next morning.

The following morning, it was early and fourteen was being ripped apart by the security guards. I just went about my business. I didn't want to be anywhere near any of this. They had their able friend, the drug dog, with them, now if there were any drugs about, he would find them, lovely spaniel.

Sixteen, which had been fired the night before, was looking a complete mess, everyone always wanted a look to see just how bad it was and I was no different; human nature, I suppose. Its entire contents had been destroyed; charred pieces of wood remained laying in the half-flooded cell. The cells are made for just an occurrence, then they are left for the relevant people to come and assess, the governor for instance, before they decide on what punishment is deemed necessary.

By the middle of the afternoon, we had gone into complete lock down, everyone was locked away, guards were absolutely everywhere searching with the drug dogs. Something wasn't right here and our day had come to a very premature end. I wasn't even allowed to go over to Education to finish any painting off. Even the governors were out searching, from what was being whispered around, all we could tell was something was either coming over the wall, or someone was trying to smuggle something in to the prison, thanks guys.

Heading into my final week here now and we have a covid outbreak, it appears that most of the inmates are clear but there is a small part of the induction wing infected and the guards are dropping quickly. At the last count, as far as we know, we have four guards with covid and seven self isolating. This has had a major impact and Sunday sees the whole prison on virtual lock down, everything is slowly grinding to a halt. They just don't have enough guards to go around and it looks like nothing will be happening today and I mean absolutely nothing.

Wouldn't you think that an organization which is run at the end of the day by a government body, might actually have a backup plan in cases of emergency, but then when you consider the lies and constant poor decision making by this conservative government, why would anybody be surprised. The so-called regime, which you would think is the back bone of the society we are living in, is lying in tatters. Madness ensues in here; dinner is like being on Noah's Ark and inmates are sent down two by two and exercise no longer exists.

There are several governors who walk the corridors of HMP Leicester. I wonder what they are doing this Sunday afternoon, they certainly don't appear to be anywhere near today. Instead of sitting at home in the garden playing happy families, perhaps they should be working the wings in here. When the going gets tough, the tough get going. I thought that was how the song went, shame on you all. The top man will be sat thinking that he has got away with his poor decision making this weekend, but deep down he knows that over the next few weeks, somebody will pay for these adolescent decisions. I wonder if he is brave enough to own up, hold up his hands and admit he actually got this wrong or will he just pass the buck. Sure, enough it didn't take long for someone upstairs to smash his cell up and have a go at the guards, you have got what you deserved, just a pity that they got off so lightly. We come back again to that saying, treat people like animals and they will behave like animals.

As the new week actually begins the barbers is finished and they have erected the old traditional barbers sign, red, white and blue spinning around. I wonder how long it will be before somebody smashes that off the wall. The Education department has received a tremendous overhaul, even if I say so myself, well somebody has to blow my trumpet. It is a fresh-looking environment for inmates to learn in, once things get back to normal and I have gone on my merry way.

CHAPTER EIGHTEEN - FINALLY HOME

My emotions are running in so many different directions, normally when you leave somewhere they throw a party and everyone says farewell. Totally different in here, certainly no party going on, you build various different relationships along this stormy road and then you either miss people who are on shifts, or bump into people on the off chance. It could actually take all week to say goodbye to the few people I would like to acknowledge and thank for their help. The other thing is I'm useless at saying goodbye; hate it, as the emotions run too deep in some cases.

Friday will be my last day over in the Education department, that could be a long goodbye with some of the staff over there. Then we move onto the Careers department, she has helped me so much in here and she usually works elsewhere on a Friday, so no doubt goodbyes could run over several days. Luckily for me, Tad has already left, which makes life much easier I was dreading leaving him in here. The rest of the lads come and go on a daily basis, so no problem with any of them. Bob my cell mate is in his own little world, tough, but only he can know why he is really here and goodbye should be fairly straight forward.

Lastly, it won't be goodbye, when I walk back through those gates and back into the real world again into the arms of my wife; it will be a great big hello and sorry. It will be like winning the lottery a million times over and much, much more. As the week trundles by, I have found guards coming up to me to say farewell and talk for ages about life in general and what lies ahead. They all want to know when I go, making sure they say farewell or just checking if they have another shift before I leave, it's all quite overwhelming.

My young lady from the Careers department was always going to be my hardest goodbye. I just couldn't handle it and I knew she wouldn't either. She had said to me previously "why did I start with you in here", I was her first sort of client I guess when she started several weeks ago. I don't know the answer but everything happens for a reason. I couldn't handle it, so I decided to write a letter to her; I'm no chicken that was the only way of handling this, but by writing it all down, I wouldn't forget anything. I popped into her office, handed her the letter and told her not to open until she had left for the day, she agreed. I said my goodbyes to her, very difficult. I said "This is not goodbye, only farewell, we will meet again one day" and I went on my way, tough one, hard to fight back the emotions, but you cannot show you are weak in here and off I went.

Friday arrives and it's my last trip over to the Education department and I had no idea what to expect, reservations ran through my mind as we approached, how would they all react with me. Would they be sorry to see me go? I think the answer was yes but nobody was showing anything. I learnt a harsh lesson today. The staff must all leave their emotions at the gate when they clock on every day. It was almost completely heartless with no feelings at all. I was shocked but it made it easier for me. It was just a polite thanks for what you have done and good luck.

There obviously we're a couple of exceptions, the young girls in the office found it very hard, just as I did, to just say bye and walk away. Normally, you would be giving each other a big hug, but that certainly wasn't happening here today. A couple of the teachers went out of their way to track me down and say goodbye, offering their hands, which was nice. One said don't worry, when we meet on the outside, I won't cross over the road; that brought a smile to my face and that was it, back to the wing.

One of the younger girls from the office came over to the wing to say a final farewell. It must be very hard for a young girl getting on so well with an inmate, having a laugh on a daily basis with a bit of banter and then having to say farewell. Tough for anybody, let alone a youngster, just finding her way in the world. I will never forget her.

The prison seems to be on a bit of a mission at the moment, clamping down on trouble makers and shipping them out to other prisons. Inmates are being moved, covid has died down and some sort of equilibrium has returned. Some unruly characters seemed to be taking over, but the guards have taken back control, not to be messed with, it would appear. They have tried to have drugs thrown over the wall into the yard, which were intercepted and binned, how happy the governor must have been with that result. The guards have also been searched on different occasions and as far as we know, one has been arrested for trying to bring mobile phones in, for inmates. It never stops.

A few weeks ago now, Tad and me got to know a young man called Bill, he was always cleaning his cell, he was OCD that was for sure but a little over the top at times. He was released and I told Tad that before I left, he would be back in here. I thought I was wrong but today I looked out over the yard where the new inmates exercise and there he is, true to form, very predictable and very, very sad. If only Tad was here to see, well maybe not.

It was now my final weekend and one of my favourite guards was on all weekend, which was great. My Saturday paper was delivered bright and early. Lots of banter going on and all seemed well in HMP Leicester. My mind was all over the place; just two more sleeps, as they say, and then free, back out in the big wide world.

The weekend was predictably very slow. I knew this would happen, it's one of those times when you just want Monday to be here. The Olympics have started, apart from which nothing really to watch on the television. Bob is in his own little world, he is on remand until January next year, looking at a possible murder charge. He is in a better place than when I first had the pleasure of his company. He now has his solicitor on the case, he has the mental health team supporting him and Education on the horizon. None of which he was chasing, but you have to make these people work for you, like I said before, they will not come knocking.

The weekends in here are dreadful and this one has been the longest I have ever known. I knew I wouldn't sleep much on Sunday night I just wanted to get out of here. I was up with the lark. Monday morning had arrived the 26th July. 5am, Olympics on the television and I started to strip my bed. Everything had to be handed back, if it needed washing it had to go off to the laundry and then I just had a pile of papers which would be all I take away from here, dos and don'ts for the next 15 weeks. I told Bob he could have everything that I had left, crisps, squash that sort of thing.

7.30am and the guard opens the door. I was just watching the final of the diving. Daley going for gold he couldn't, could he. She said "Beresford, 30 minutes, be ready". Now let me think about that for a moment. Be ready. I think I might just manage that. True to her word 8am and she is back. Daley has one dive left though. Oh well catch up at home. It wasn't difficult saying goodbye to Bob, we never really got that close, we wished each other well and I was ready for the walk back to freedom.

Guards who were starting the day shift were shouting bye and I shouted to the two remaining lads from Vietnam. Out of the wing into the fresh air and a delightful walk back to the reception area, only this time it was the opposite. Four of us were escorted, two lads going to court and another lad and me to be released. It was just after 8am and I had told my wife 9am so I let the other lad go in front of me. The other two lads and me were placed back in the original cell when this all started, back in April.

The guard came about 8.15 for the two lads to go to court. I was all alone for my final 15 minutes or so in this hell hole, although

I'm sure this is not the worst prison in the world. I sat reflecting on what was about to happen, then the door opened "come on Beresford let's get you out of here". I was asked to change back into my own clothes and I was handed a sack for the dirty washing. Then approaching the desk to be handed back my mobile phone and release documents, along with some cash to tide me over.

Then the final walk, back through the original door where I met the black Labrador and along to the main gates. More guards appeared, who I knew, shouting and wishing me well. More questions from the guard in charge, just the same as what I had just been asked. Through a wire gate and then I stand before two large old wooden gates, like you would find at a castle, with a wooden side door.
"This is it Beresford, take care, goodbye".

The gate was opened and I walked through to the other side. I just stood there and tried to breathe.
Traffic was passing by, cars, lorries, vans, buses and people just going about their daily business. It was only 8.30 and I had to wait for my wife. I phoned her twice before I left saying no rush, 9am be perfect, idiot. Well, what can I do now, so I toddled over to the bus shelter outside of the prison and just sat and waited.

I was free and it felt amazing. Then I saw her walking up the road, the sun was shining and her hair was blowing in the early morning breeze. She was a good 100 metres away, I stood up from the bus shelter, our eyes met, finally hugs and kisses after all those visits when we had absolutely no contact. Time to make up for lost time, we separated, I took her hand and we walked off together to begin the rest of our lives as one.